# MASKS OF THE SOUL

An up-to-date, critical examination of the concept of reincarnation.

*By the same author*

BEYOND THE BODY

ENCYCLOPEDIA OF ESOTERIC MAN

ENCYCLOPEDIA OF METAPHYSICAL MEDICINE

HINDU WORLD

SEX AND THE SUPERNATURAL

# MASKS OF THE SOUL

## The Facts Behind Reincarnation

*by*

BENJAMIN WALKER

THE AQUARIAN PRESS
Wellingborough, Northamptonshire

First published 1981





British Library Cataloguing in Publication Data
Walker, Benjamin
Masks of the soul.
1. Reincarnation 2. Psychical research
I. Title
133.9'01'3 BF1311.R35

ISBN 0-85030-259-5
ISBN 0-85030-258-7 Pbk

Typeset by Ad'House, Northamptonshire.
Printed by Nene Litho, Earls Barton,
and bound by Weatherby Woolnough,
Wellingborough, Northamptonshire.

# Contents

# Preface

The purpose of this book is to provide the reader with the essential facts relevant to a proper understanding of the fascinating and controversial subject of reincarnation.

Any acceptance of the thesis involves certain presuppositions and raises certain problems which must therefore be considered from the outset. Thus, we cannot accept reincarnation unless we acknowledge the existence of the soul and believe in its immortality. Again, one must make a distinction between the temporary mask we call the personality, which perishes at death along with the physical body, and the soul which survives it.

It is also necessary to consider the purpose of reincarnation, traditionally expressed in terms of the operation of karma, the law of action and reaction, which explains the process and provides a metaphysical rationale for the theory.

Belief in reincarnation has a long history, and this is briefly reviewed, in order to show how widespread it has been and how tenacious its hold on the imagination of all peoples, past and present.

In presenting the case for reincarnation every major argument in support of the theory has been advanced, so as to furnish a satisfactory basis for the belief. In this century alone there have been literally hundreds of cases of alleged reincarnation, many of which have been investigated by experienced researchers. It is obviously not possible to analyse or even mention all of them, and I have therefore confined myself to a few 'classics' among the more recent case histories, which I have described briefly, adding some critical comments.

Against all this I have set the ideas of those who find the

theory unacceptable for various reasons, and who have presented alternative hypotheses, providing explanations that in their view account adequately for the evidence brought forward by advocates of the doctrine.

It can be said of reincarnation that the testimony of tradition is in its favour, while scientific evidence is against it. We therefore cannot be so sceptical as to reject it outright, nor so dogmatic as to accept it without qualification. This book presents the evidence from both sides, and it is left to readers to draw their own conclusions.

The bibliography appended to this work gives a fairly comprehensive list, with publication details, of the chief books on the subject, a few of which deserve special mention. John Hick's book on death and eternal life provides a valuable survey of the philosophical background, and contains some scholarly chapters on reincarnation. Also useful are the collected statements of famous people expressing their belief in the doctrine, such as the compilations made by E.D. Walker and Eva Martin, and in particular the excellent anthology edited by Joseph Head and S.L. Cranston, which includes quotations from the world's religious writings, and from over 400 poets, philosophers, novelists, psychiatrists and others.

To readers interested in modern examples of reincarnation the works of the following are recommended, both for the information they provide and for the many useful comments made by the authors on the cases considered by them: Thomas Sugrue and Noel Langley for Edgar Cayce: Morey Bernstein and Milton Kline for Bridey Murphy; Joan Grant, Gina Cerminara, Martin Ebon, Arthur Guirdham, Jess Stearn, Edward Ryall, Jeffrey Iverson, and above all, Ian Stevenson. The books by Peter Underwood and Leonard Wilder, and Peter Moss and Joe Keeton, bring the list of principal sources virtually up to the minute.

I must record my indebtedness to Derek Jones, M.A., F.L.A., Borough Librarian at Richmond Upon Thames, and Philip Rayner, District Librarian, Teddington, through whose kindness I was provided with the opportunity of consulting scores of books that I was unable to obtain from the usual sources. The courtesy and helpfulness of the staff at these libraries is also gratefully acknowledged, in particular, Sheila Turner, Jane Blackmore, Jane Clement, and Terence Daily.

B.W.
Teddington

# 1
# Man and His Destiny

When in February 1848 the eighty-year old John Quincy Adams, sixth President of the United States, was dying, he said, 'This is the last of earth. I am content'. Whatever other implications this statement may have had, it is generally taken as expressing the belief that he was finally to be rid of his mundane concerns.

Yet the last of earth is not what a large part of the world's population would accept as the inevitable consequence of death. The novelist Katherine Mansfield expressed another view: 'The only thing to do is to get the dying over, to court it almost, and then all hands to the business of being reborn again'.

People who accept the theory of reincarnation believe that the souls of those who have died return in another bodily form after a period of bodiless existence in some region beyond, and continue to return again and again for repeated trials and probations until their shortcomings are corrected, and they attain perfection.

As day follows night, and night is succeeded by day, so runs the sequence of birth-death-rebirth. The soul of man is bound to the cycle of successive embodiments. Our present life is therefore to be seen as one of a long series of lives, and the particular entity we are in our present life is one of a chain of separate entities inhabited by the identical soul, sent repeatedly to earth to complete its schooling and purification. Sir Rider Haggard, author of *She*, the well-known reincarnation novel, wrote, 'The Personality [soul] which animates each one of us is immeasurably ancient, having been forged in many fires'.

In order to understand a little more fully the further implications of reincarnation we shall have to examine the constitution and nature of man himself.

### Somatic and Asomatic Elements

In a broad sense, the elements that contribute to making the human being what he is can be put into two groups. Firstly, the somatic (Gk. *soma*, 'body') elements, concerned with the bodily organism, whose composition and functioning can be explained in terms of physics and chemistry. Secondly, the asomatic or non-physical elements that include the personality, the psyche and the soul.

The study of the asomatic side of the human entity is beset with difficulties because it is intangible. Some scientists in fact deny the existence of any such elements. Yet this intangible part of man forms the basis of such studies as psychology, metaphysics, religion, mysticism and the occult. The many terms used for the various aspects of the asoma are shadowy, vague and difficult to define: the mind, astral body, prana, personality, etheric body, self, soul, spirit, ego, psyche, atman. Each religion and each culture has its own classification and its own nomenclature, often confused, imprecise and overlapping.

Perhaps a clearer picture will be gained if we consider what might be called the history of the soul. This history may be said to have started with the vibratory impulse by which the entire phenomenal universe came into existence when, as the Bible picturesquely puts it, God said, 'Let there be light'.

Each created unit in the universe is an ent, an entity or energy unit. All units, from molecule to animal, are ents. The lesser elements within the larger, such as the cells within the body, also in their way constitute independent ents. All such units, including the so-called inanimate and insentient units of matter, are said to have a degree of life and a degree of awareness.

This idea was accepted by many early societies, and is known as animism, that is, that each separate thing possesses an *anima*, an active nucleus of mind-energy, and is a life-and-mind 'organism'. Once regarded as a primitive notion, animism has also been seriously considered as a scientific proposition by modern thinkers. The German philosopher Friedrich von Schelling wrote, 'Mind sleeps in stone, dreams in the plant, awakes in the animal, and becomes conscious in man'.

All objects and living things in the universe may thus be graded in an ascending series of increasingly complex animas. The underlying essence of the elementary object such as a stone was called the *anima materia*, a form of primitive mind-energy with only dormant awareness. The proto-consciousness of the anima materia is unformed, immature, untested, inexperienced, in the lower range of evolution, and lacking in a spiritual identity.

The life-and-mind anima that is believed to inhere in stone is found in a greater degree of complexity in the plant kingdom (*anima herba*), and reaches a still higher degree in the animal kingdom (*anima bruta*). In the animal stage of development the anima is carnal and instinctive. The animal has an etheric body, and possesses what the Greeks called *pneuma*, and the Hindus *jiva*, both words meaning 'breath' and also 'life'.

The human entity in turn possesses all the anima elements that are found in material ents, in plants and in animals. But in the human being these factors are attuned to evolve more specifically into what is called the personality, a word derived from the Latin *persona*, or 'mask'.

### The Personality and the Psyche

In the Buddhist view the personality may be regarded as the *nama-rupa*, the 'name-and-shape' part of the human being, a transient aspect of the more enduring psyche. The personality is the creation of the parental and ancestral biological inheritance, and is conditioned by its social environment. It is an incidental experiment for the widening experience of the individual soul.

The empirical or experiencing person, the Buddhist name-and-shape, commits deeds, and because of these deeds another name-and-shape is born after its death. When physical life ends, these superficial accretions of the individual that make up his personality will be discarded. This concept plays an important part in the doctrine of reincarnation.

As the personality is associated with the name-and-shape of the individual, so the psyche is associated with his mind-and-thought element and his astral body. The psyche is the central directorate of the individual and his innermost moral self. It is the enduring and evolving nucleus of the human entity, which integrates, co-ordinates and gives continuing identity to the human being. The astral body survives the death of the physical body, and the disintegration of the etheric body and the personality.

The Greek writer Plutarch (d. A.D. 120), a philosopher, historian, moralist and mathematician, who travelled widely and held public office as consul under the emperor Trajan, and who was later initiated into the ancient mysteries to become high priest at the famous temple of Delphi, gives us a description of the two higher asomatic (non-physical) elements in man as they had been communicated to him.

They are the psyche or human-soul, and the *nous* or divine-soul kernel. The latter is described as an invisible cord-like shape positioned immediately above the head. The lower end of the cord touches and is slightly submerged within the skull. This lower end constitutes the psyche or human soul of the individual, and is identical with what the medieval scholastics called the *anima humana*. It is the point of contact between matter and spirit. In some accounts the anima humana is treated as the seat or envelope of the divine soul.

The condition and appearance of the psyche, says Plutarch, are determined by the vices of the body and the passions of the mind. Some psyches are like clear moonlight, of marvellous purity, but others are scratched, tainted and discoloured, sometimes mottled like adders, sometimes tattered like old garments.

There exist various ancient traditions regarding the ultimate destiny of the psyche. Some say that the condition of the psyche determines whether the incorruptible *nous* will remain with it after the death of the body. If the psyche is pure it will accompany the *nous* to immortality. If unworthy it will be left to the corruption and dissolution it has earned. Others hold that the *nous* is on loan to the psyche, and by its good conduct this loan may become a permanent endowment. Man has the privilege of gaining immortality and participating in eternal life.

In modern terms, as the personality affects the psyche, so the psyche affects the overself. Like the ever-handsome Dorian Gray in Oscar Wilde's story, we may live out our lives oblivious of the consequences of our thoughts and actions, yet all the time the portrait in the attic is undergoing a slow transmutation into a horrible decay as it bears the marks of the hero's dissolute life.

**The Soul**

Finally, we come to the overself or soul, known to the scholastics as the *anima divina*, the highest of the non-physical elements in the human being. It is the pre-existent divine element in man. Just as psychologists have at times denied the existence of mind (*see* Ryle, 1949), so materialists, atheists and humanists deny the existence of the soul, or any form of personal survival. According to them, when a man dies he is extinguished, permanently and for ever, and that is all there is to it. Any talk of the soul is foolish and meaningless.

Yet, in the opinion of many eminent thinkers, the premiss that there is some underlying entity that gives unity to our complex make-up and direction to our existence, accounting for our personal and social idealism, our moral aspirations, our yearning for self-improvement, is a difficult one to resist. All these would seem to represent, they feel, the impulse of some indwelling principle towards its divine origin. A timeless element, says Plato must exist in man to respond to the timeless concepts of truth, beauty and goodness. In Biblical terms, faith, hope and charity are not attributes of the material part of our earthly heritage, but of the eternal soul.

Knowledge of the soul cannot be derived from reason, observation or science, or from any field of human learning. It cannot be compared with the brain or heart, with breath or blood. It cannot be equated with biological life, with consciousness, instinct or emotion. It is unique. Sometimes it is identified with man's conscience, the inner monitor that enables him to distinguish right from wrong. But conscience is to some degree the product of one's birth and upbringing and cannot be entirely equated with the soul.

While no sexual element can be assigned to the soul, it is described in the way that God is, as androgynous, being both male and female, and therefore single, unified and complete.

The soul is the most mysterious and least known part of man. The Swiss psychologist Carl Gustav Jung (d. 1961) called it 'the greatest of all cosmic miracles'. It does not belong to man; man belongs to the soul. It is divinely conceived, without form, wholly spiritual, and is by nature religious. The reality of its existence may be known through divine grace, mystical insight, prophetic revelation or intuitive understanding, and to most people its acceptance is an act of faith.

Basic to the concept of the soul is the fact that it is immortal, and that the individual entity is a flame fed from an eternal divine fire. And since the soul can have no temporal beginning, its pre-existence must be assumed. Originally and long before the soul became embodied on earth it had its being in what is thought of variously as the universal soul, the divine mind or some transcendent non-material sphere. The soul belongs to a continuum, without beginning and without end. Lafcadio Hearn, American writer of Irish-Greek birth wrote, 'The substance of the Self is older than the sun'. It is an indestructible particle that endures for ever. It does not perish, either here or hereafter.

Belief in some form of personal survival is found in all societies with any kind of religious faith. Sir James Frazer, lifelong student of early religions and folklore wrote, 'The question whether one's conscious personality survives after death has been answered by almost all races of man in the affirmative'.

The ideas of the pre-existence and the immortality of the soul are bound together. As death will not be the end, so birth was not a beginning. There was never a time when the soul was not, and there never will come a time when it shall cease to be. The soul was in existence before the birth of the body and will continue to exist after the death of the body.

Even the sceptic sometimes doubts the validity of his own opinions, when he reflects on the problems of life and death. Robert Green Ingersoll, rationalist, agnostic and critic of religious faith, could not always sustain his belief in the non-existence of the soul. Speaking on the occasion of a child's death he said, 'We do not know whether the grave is the end of this life, or the door of another, or whether the night here is not somewhere else a dawn... The dead do not suffer. If they live again, their lives will surely be as good as ours... We [Agnostics] too, have a religion, and it is this: help for the living – hope for the dead' (Head and Cranston, 1961, p.243).

Man sometimes has a profound sense of the soul's immortality, an intimate awareness that part of his being is deathless. The body perishes, but the soul lives on. All the experience and wisdom he has acquired, he feels, cannot just be cast into the void when he dies. He is certain that his religious hopes and spiritual aspirations will somewhere be fulfilled.

The almost universal desire to believe in the soul's immortality perhaps rests on man's own yearning for immortality, a yearning which itself would imply the existence of a reality to fulfil this yearning. James Martineau, the great English theologian said, 'We do not believe in immortality because we have proved it, but we forever try to prove it because we believe it'.

Belief in immortality follows from a belief in some supreme power above us. For man, the one is meaningless without the other. Without God and immortality this life becomes a much-ado-about-nothing mission. The English historian Henry Thomas Buckle wrote, 'If immortality be untrue, it matters little whether anything else be true or not'. In the words of the Basque poet Miguel Unamuno, 'What is it to me whether God exists, unless I can live for ever'.

We can now summarize the chief elements of the asomatic or non-physical part of the human being. These can conveniently be reduced to three, namely: (a) the transient name-and-shape personality, (b) the evolving mind-psyche, and (c) the immortal soul-kernel.

These three elements were known to the Greeks as the pneuma, psyche, *nous*. To the Hindus as jiva, prana, atman. To the Chinese as p'o, hun and ch'i. To the Jews as nefesh, ruah, neshama. To the medieval scholastics as anima bruta, anima humana, anima divina. To the occultist as the etheric body, the astral body, the soul (*see* tabulation).

As the personality is concerned with life, instincts, senses and egos, so the psyche is concerned with the emotional, intellectual and moral side of life, and the soul with the spiritual sphere. The first is associated with brain consciousness, the second with the higher collective unconscious, and the soul with universal consciousness. The first is referred to in Buddhist tradition as the name-and-shape, the second is the reasoning mind-and-thought of the medieval schoolmen, the third equated with the Idea-and-Form of Plato. The first belongs to the passing world of shadows, the second to the potential world of becoming, the third to the permanent world of Being. The evolution of the individual is an advance from ego, through self to Essence.

Reincarnationists take up the tale of the soul's history in their own way. Although they differ on some points they are in general agreement in saying that the material environment is necessary for the development of the essential self (call it psyche or soul). Through the material medium, they say, the soul is brought into contact with a dimension necessary for its progress. It is only here that a certain essential stage of biological evolution, with its accompanying psychological perception and spiritual awareness, can best be reached.

The aboriginal, undeveloped soul we had on first incarnation is 'civilised' through centuries and millennia of experience in varying grades of cultural advancement in various historical epochs and social situations. There is a purpose in every life. The rich man is perhaps being rewarded; the poor man is perhaps being punished; both are being tested.

The soul grows and is perfected through the body and psyche, a long process requiring the schooling of more than one lifetime in bodily form. The identical soul animates a plurality of bodies, and continues from life to life to acquire a wider and wider range of knowledge. It retains a continuing, if unconscious, memory of its successive lives, and it is prompted and guided by, and is in effect the product of, its many past selves.

The current personality allotted to the soul for a particular round of existence is one of many personalities that are put on during the soul's successive journeys through the world, and is an incidental experiment for the widening experience, through the psyche, of that particular soul. The soul is constant, the venue changes.

Professor C.J. Ducasse, formerly president of the American Philosophical Association, suggested that one should take one's personality with a large grain of salt. The personality is a fiction, participating in a masquerade, for in each incarnation the evolving psyche assumes a new personality, just as an actor wears a different costume and assumes a different name as he performs for an hour or two upon the stage a different role in a different play, once the Prince of Denmark, once Shylock, once Othello. In the theatre where these dramas are enacted the ephemeral personalities come and go like phantoms, and when their part is played the masks are cast aside. So after each incarnation the personality, the outward image a man presents to the world, will disappear like a shadow without a body, but the soul will proceed to its next role. The shape alters, the Form remains.

**The asomatic or non-physical elements of the human being**

| | PERSONALITY | MIND | SOUL |
|---|---|---|---|
| Greek | pneuma | psyche | nous |
| Hindu | jiva | prana | atman |
| Chinese | p'o | hun | ch'i |
| Jewish | nefesh | ruah | neshama |
| Church scholastics | anima bruta | anima humana | anima divina |
| Type of self | ego-self | higher self | Overself or Essence |
| Associated metaphysical concept | name-shape | mind-thought | Idea-Form |
| Occult correspondence | etheric body | astral body | soul |
| Sphere of control | life, senses, instincts | emotions, intellect | spirit |
| Mental plane | conscious | collective unconscious | universal consciousness |
| Governing law | natural | moral | spiritual |
| World of operation | illusions or shadows | becoming | Being |
| Destiny | transient | potential or evolving | permanent or immortal |

**Reasons for Re-embodiment**

The premiss of reincarnation being conceded, a number of reasons have been put forward by different religious schools to explain what causes the souls of those who have died to be embodied in material form again. We shall consider some of the more important ones.

In some gnostic systems rebirth on this earth is seen as an expiation for a mythological crime, like original sin, committed by an ancestor of the community or a remote progenitor of the human race (Eisler, 1921, p.2). Reincarnation may also be personally punitive. The sinner must face retribution, so that his past iniquities may be absolved by due punishment in another birth. It provides a chance for restitution for those souls who have done harm to others, enabling them to make amends for the errors of their past lives. This is implicit in the doctrine of karma, the law of cause and consequence, which will be considered in greater detail later.

Further, reincarnation may be sought by souls in order to fulfil an unfinished task, or to complete an uncompleted mission. According to the Zohar, a medieval compendium of Hebrew theosophy, those who are unmarried, or die without issue, must be 'planted anew' to produce progeny.

It may provide another chance for souls who have sunk so low in the moral scale as to lose all hope of advancement on the spiritual plane. F.W.H. Myers, the famous psychical researcher, communicating from the other side after death, spoke of reincarnation as necessary for 'animal men'.

Again, those for whom incarnation has been a failure, such as the aborted child, the still-born child, the congenital idiot, those who died in childhood with their lives unfulfilled, or those whose lives were cut short by murder or suicide, or who otherwise died a violent death, are reincarnated in order to complete the term of their natural lives.

Reincarnation provides the soul with the opportunity to savour as many and as varied experiences as possible, to accomplish different tasks in different lives, so that it might have the widest scope for progress. Bit by bit, in the course of several lifetimes, the virtues are cultivated, errors eliminated, the soul evolves, and acquires a kind of universal wisdom and perfection.

Finally, an earthly life may be assumed by spirits of supreme degree, or by advanced souls who have attained the highest merit and achieved supreme enlightenment, who decide to forgo final liberation and choose to return so that they might help, instruct and liberate suffering humanity. Such are the *bodhisattvas* or saviour-beings of Buddhism.

According to Hinduism the fundamental cause and purpose of reincarnation is *karma*, a Sanskrit word meaning 'action', here implying both action and reaction. It refers specifically to the continuing and far-reaching effects of what one does in life. The nearest equivalent is probably found in the concept of retribution, a word that comes from the Latin term meaning 'giving in return'. As the Bible has it, 'Whatsoever a man soweth, that shall he also reap' (Gal. 6.7).

The same idea is latent in the Greek *heimarmenē*, 'destiny', implying also 'deserts', which is the inescapable chain of cause and effect resulting from personal behaviour and divine decision, that brings upon a man his share of reward and punishment.

Even science admits a kind of karmic law, the scientific substitutes being 'causality', and the 'laws of nature'. For every action there is an equal and opposite reaction. This law is also found to operate in society, where the legal and social systems mete out in their own fashion the rewards and punishments for dutiful, courageous or criminal behaviour.

Karma is the principle of universal causality, perpetuated by one's actions. Every thought, word, deed and desire, has a dynamic quality, producing good or bad results. Some simple act of charity may change a life or mould a destiny. Actions give rise to effects, and the sum total of these actions determines the nature, character, status and circumstances of happiness or misery of a person in his next life, and so on from incarnation to incarnation.

If a person has lived virtuously and endeavoured to throw off his weaknesses and imperfections, he is given a new life of comfort and happiness. If he was evil, he is born to a life of suffering and wretchedness. In other words, every person lives in a world that he has earned, a world of his own making. Punishment and reward may not come immediately, but come they will.

The doctrine of karma holds that there is no escape from the universal law of cause and consequence. Over-indulgence in one life means a hangover in the next. In one's present existence one is haunted by the ghosts of one's previous life. By one's good deeds one accumulates capital, by one's evil deeds one adds to the deficit. The karmic accounting is exact. Any deficiency or surplus is carried over in the ledgers for future reckoning by the karmic auditors.

Some authorities hold that the actions for which a man is accountable are only those that are meant or intended, whether for good or evil. It is primarily the motive that determines whether an action is karma-bearing. A person is therefore not accountable for his unconscious acts, his involuntary thoughts, or his dreams.

But from the strictly orthodox standpoint this concession is not warranted. To live is to act and think, and all actions and thoughts, whatever their source, carry a karma-content. Modern psychology seems to confirm this rigid view. According to the Freudians there is a concealed motivation even in our inadvertencies, in our mistakes and casual errors. St Augustine (d. 430), aware that his dreams could not bear close inspection, thanked God that he was not responsible for them. But according to the psychologists he was in error. We are responsible for our dreams. They are a picturization of our hidden desires. They reflect the portrait in the attic.

Karma involves the soul's sojourn on earth, then an interlude, brief or extended, in the next world, followed by the journey back to earth again. This migration of the soul, this process of re-embodiment, this cycle of coming and going, is known in Sanskrit as *samsara*, 'flowing', signifying the ceaseless motion to and fro in the ocean of births and deaths.

In this manner the soul must continue to inhabit body after body until the stage is reached when, untainted by imperfection, and with no residue of karma left, it earns its final release from rebirth and attains *moksha*, 'deliverance', never more to return to its earthly pilgrimage. When moksha is achieved the *atman* or personal soul is in a state of beatitude, and is absorbed into Brahma, the universal soul, as a drop of rain water merges into the sea.

**The Post-Death Experience**

Several subsidiary questions arise from the theory of reincarnation. What happens after death? Does everyone reincarnate? How often does any individual soul have to reincarnate? What length of time elapses between incarnations? Do we always return to earth in human form or do we sometimes come back as birds or animals? Why do we not remember our previous incarnate existence? Why do we forget the time spent between death and rebirth?

It is generally accepted that on the death of the body, the soul, spirit or psyche becomes a kind of disembodied mind, a bodiless consciousness. Most religions speak of a Judgment, when the soul is brought before a tribunal and its merits and demerits examined and considered, and judgment passed. The virtuous are sent to heaven, the evil to hell.

In the reincarnationist view, the soul in the intercarnate condition, called in Tibetan Buddhism the *bardo* or 'between' state, and popularly and inaccurately equated with 'pre-existence', resides in a non-earthly sphere for longer or shorter periods. Except for those rare souls that have achieved perfection, every soul is rewarded for its virtues, and every soul punished for its sins. The crop of rewards and punishments is reaped in the various planes of heaven and hell, where the rights and wrongs of earthly behaviour are demonstrated to it by joyous or painful experiences. It has been said that a man is punished by his sins, and not for them; he is rewarded by his virtues and not because of them.

But the distinctive feature of the reincarnationist view is that heaven, hell or purgatory, do not erase the effects of karma. Karma can only be 'worked out' on the material plane, that is, on earth, which is therefore called *karma-bhumi*, or 'karma-place'. The possibility of reincarnation on other planetary or even stellar systems has sometimes been suggested, but this is not the general view. It is on earth that one creates karma, and it is to earth that one must return to cancel it out. When a soul has recieved the full measure of its reward or punishment in heaven or hell, it returns to another body on earth.

In many primitive societies it was widely believed that only important tribal personages reincarnated, after spending some time with the great ancestors, and after a certain number of such incarnations became 'ancestors' themselves. The lesser members of the tribe when they died, remained below in the spirit regions and never returned to the earth plane. But in the Hindu and Buddhist belief everyone reincarnates, and continues to do so until he attains spiritual perfection. Modern reincarnationists generally hold to the latter view.

On the other hand, there are some who believe that reincarnation is not universal, but may be optional, and that there is an element of personal choice in the matter. William Thomas Stead, a well-known writer of his day, and champion of spiritualism, who was drowned in the *Titanic* disaster, was said to have communicated with his daughter after his death. In one message he stated that those with a good record can choose whether to return to earth or not. Those with a poor record do not qualify for choice and are directed to return to earth (Cannon, 1970, p.44).

The time spent by the soul in the intercarnate condition is differently given as well, and seems to vary from culture to culture. In places where reincarnation is the accepted belief, life is said to succeed life very rapidly, usually within one to ten years. The Jains of India and some Tibetan Buddhists believe in almost instantaneous reincarnation. Some believe that as the soul progresses the waiting period becomes longer and longer. Many modern exponents in the West state that the interval between incarnations may span decades, or even centuries.

### The Return of the Soul

For its return, the soul has to await an opportune moment. According to the Buddhists, at the allotted time the soul has a vision of a mating couple, its future parents, and descends into the woman's womb on conception. According to the Kabalists, the soul awaiting reincarnation is summoned before a heavenly tribunal and ordered to go back to earth. Though it is reluctant to be born again it has no choice but to obey. While the would-be parents are engaged in intercourse the astral outline of the forthcoming body that will house the soul gradually takes shape and hovers over them. If the couple were permitted to see it they would perceive above their heads an image resembling a human face, and it is in this image that the child will be formed. Sexual union does not create an immortal soul. It only prepares a material habitation for it.

Just before the soul enters the womb the memory of its past earthly life and its intercarnate state is extinguished. This is symbolically described in different traditions. In Chinese Buddhism when the soul is ready for reincarnation, the presiding goddess of the underworld, Meng P'o, offers the soul a drink of bitter-sweet broth, which blots out from its memory all knowledge of what has gone before. In his *Republic*, Plato (d. 347 B.C.) also states that souls about to be reborn drink of the river Lethe (Greek, 'forgetfulness') so that all they knew is erased from their minds. Similarly, the Kabalists say that the night-angel Layela gives the hovering soul a little pinch on the nose coupled with a light pressure on its upper lip, which makes it forget everything it knows. We are all said to bear the mark of the angel's finger on our lips.

The question of the form in which we return to the material plane has also been variously answered. It is generally agreed that the kind of body we have depends on the way the soul has acquitted itself in the previous life. Certain eastern systems teach that we may reincarnate as lower animal species. This is called *transmigration*, 'moving across' from one form to another, or *metensomatosis*, change in body.

In popular Buddhism the sinful and unrepentant are reborn as animals, or else condemned to roam as hungry ghosts or earth-bound spirits. Peter Underwood cites the case of the Ceylonese villagers who refused to help Sri Lanka's Archaeological Department to drive off a swarm of hornets near an ancient fortress during excavations because they believed the insects to be the reincarnated soldiers of King Kassapa (*c.* A.D. 495) who had once occupied the fortress.

The last section of the compendium of laws by the Hindu legislator Manu (*c.* 500 B.C.) is concerned with the 'fruits of karma', according to which the soul enters a particular womb in the present life as a result of what it has done in a previous birth. The brahmin (a member of the highest caste) who drinks intoxicating liquor will become a bird that lives on ordure; the man who kills a brahmin will enter the womb of a she-ass or sow; the thief will become a lizard or rat, and so on.

The number of incarnations in each case is likewise said to be determined by the progress of the individual soul. Man's soul has a vast and almost infinite task, that of perfecting itself, and this cannot be accomplished in the course of a single brief lifetime or in one corporeal form. It needs to be incarnated many times to fulfil its destiny. It must live as a man and as a woman, know poverty and wealth, success and failure, sickness, happiness, frustration, pleasure, degradation, ecstasy, suffering, and all the other conditions that comprise the gamut of human experience.

The Greek historian Herodotus (d. 525 B.C.) wrote that according to the ancient Egyptians the soul has first to pass through the experiences of the chief forms of terrestrial, aquatic and aerial existence before it can return to animate a human form (De Vesme, 1931, p.23). In Hindu and Buddhist belief each individual reincarnates many thousands of times. Certain spiritualists say that the average person may live seven times as a man and seven as a woman, in situations that provide the soul with as many experiences as possible.

It has further been said that some evil deeds add up to such an extent that it may not be possible for the soul to bear their consequences, or even to understand their full implication, until it has had time to evolve and mature through many incarnations. Also, it may be that a particular spiritual taint can only be removed in association with the victim of one's past wrong, and the soul will have to wait for time and circumstance to bring the two together again in some future rebirth. It can happen that many incarnations will have to intervene and retribution may be held in abeyance before such a situation arises.

# 2
# History of Reincarnation

Belief in reincarnation has had an almost universal diffusion. It is found in societies both ancient and modern, both simple and sophisticated.

The idea that the dead are reborn within their own families was deeply rooted in the traditions of preliterate and primitive peoples in tropical Africa, in New Guinea, in the Pacific Islands, in Indonesia and Malaysia. It was equally widespread among the Arunta, Warramunga and other Australian aborigines. In some cases the tribal diviner could tell whose spirit was reincarnated in a newborn child.

In the New World it was found among the many indigenous Amerindian tribes, as well as among the great pre-Columbian peoples, notably the Incas of Peru. Among the Eskimos, various tribal communities of northwestern Alaska, the Aleuts of the west, and the Tlingit Indians to the southeast, also base their religious tenets on the idea of successive rebirths.

The same was true of most of the advanced nations of earlier times. According to the ancient Egyptians the dead were judged at the court of the god Osiris, and if found guilty of serious crimes were devoured by the hippopotamus or crocodile deity. The good on the other hand entered into the great hall of the gods and were regarded as *sen*, that is, belonging to the divine brotherhood. In time they were reborn as priests, kings or scribes.

The Egyptian *Book of the Dead*, extracts from which were inscribed on parchment and buried with the deceased, contains magical spells to give power to the dead to be transformed into 'whatever form they please'; a hawk, lotus, heron, sycamore, lily or phoenix. At the end of 3000 years, after transmigrating from species to species, they were finally able to make themselves a new body and be reborn in it as human beings.

**Zoroastrianism**

The religion of Zoroaster (*c.* 800 B.C.) prophet of ancient Persia, was fundamentally dualistic. It exalted Ahura Mazda, the god of light, who was in eternal opposition to Ahriman the god of darkness. Later Zoroastrianism also advanced the doctrine of reincarnation. Thus, it was said, 'In each succeeding birth the great Mazda gives to him who seeks his favour by good deeds, the gift of greater self-knowledge and greater self-control. But unto him who acts not well, but ill, he gives a worse fate in each following life'.

If during its earthly life the soul does not purify itself, remains ignorant, and seeks only the desires of the flesh, it must return and take physical bodies one after another, until it is quite pure. The good return as kings or prime ministers, or in other ways attain to high office and wealth.

Zoroastrian principles formed the basis of the middle eastern cult of Mithras, a deity of light and a powerful ally of Ahura Mazda in his struggle against Ahriman. Mithraism was brought to Rome in the first century B.C., and spread rapidly throughout the empire, including Britain, where Mithraic temples were raised from London to York. It became the official state religion of the Roman empire by decree of the emperor Aurelian (d. A.D. 275), and exerted a strong influence on Christianity and on various gnostic sects that flourished around the Mediterranean.

Another important dualistic sect to emerge under the influence of Zoroastrianism was that founded by Mani (d. A.D. 276) of Ecbatana, in southern Mesopotamia. Manichaeism taught both the pre-existence of the soul and reincarnation, the latter a process by which the imperfect light-particles in individual souls progress in successive lives to the eternal Realm of Light. St Augustine (d. A.D. 430) was a Manichaean before he became a Christian.

**Hinduism and Buddhism**

Reincarnation is of course fundamental to Hinduism, and in its earlier form was inseperable from the concept of caste. In accordance with the laws of karma the virtuous man was born into a higher caste, the wicked one into a lower caste. Ancient Hindu writings, such as the Upanishads (*c.* 650 B.C.) make numerous references to the subject. Thus, one Upanishad, the *Brihad Aranyaka*, states, 'According to a man's works and the path he goes, so a man becomes. He who does righteously becomes righteous. He who does evil becomes evil'. Another Upanishad, the *Chhandogya*, says, 'Those whose conduct here has been good will quickly attain a good birth as a brahmin or other superior caste. But those whose conduct has been evil will have an evil birth as a dog, a pig, or an untouchable outcaste.'

In the *Bhagavadgita* (*c.* A.D.300) the god Krishna tells his interlocutor Arjuna, 'Many are my lives that are past, and yours also, Arjuna. I know them all, although you are not aware of them.' The text repeatedly lays emphasis on caste, and on caste duties, with the promise of a good birth and superior status for the virtuous. 'The righteous one goes to the realms of the righteous where he dwells for an immensity of years and is then born again on earth in a good family. He who strives with all his might by efforts continued through many births, reaches at last the supreme goal.' And this supreme goal means union with the universal essence.

Buddhist metaphysics does not, strictly speaking, admit the existence of the soul as such, though in popular Buddhism the coming and going of the soul in successive rebirths is almost universally assumed. The origin of the cycle of coming and going is not explicitly made known.

In the Buddhist view man is composed of five psycho-physical elements, namely: the body, sensations, perceptions, volitions, and consciousness. These constitute what are called the five *skandhas* (Sanskrit, 'aggregates'), and it is this complex of qualities that produces *trishna* (Sanskrit, 'desire') and carries the karma of the individual. The psychic residue of the skandhas adheres to the spiritual part of the entity and is responsible for its reincarnation.

Buddhism's essential aim is to achieve liberation from the endless cycle of rebirth, and reach a state of *nirvana* ('un-feveredness'), which consists essentially in detachment from the fretful pull of desire. If the individual is not so liberated he continues to be born and reborn again and again, transmigrating from one existence to another.

Only when a man is perfect is he released from *samsara*, the ceaseless ebb and flow of birth and death. 'That man is an *arhat* (Sanskrit, 'worthy') or wise one', says a Buddhist text, 'who knows his former lives, who has known heaven and hell, and has at last reached the end of all his births.'

In Buddhist tradition Buddha himself had lived hundreds of times before he appeared as the Wise One known to history. He was in turn a peasant, slave, woman, king, bird, animal. The stories of these previous incarnations are told in the collection of tales called the *Jatakas*, which describe some 550 of Buddha's former lives. The historical Buddha (d. 483 B.C.) was the last of a series of entities that came and went on the earthly scene. In the distant future another Buddha will appear, and his name will be Maitreya.

In the Buddhist scriptures we read of Buddha saying, 'If I desire, I can by means of *deva*-vision ('god-sight') recall my many former lives, up to ten, a hundred, a thousand, a hundred thousand lives, or even more. I can give my experiences both happy and unhappy, and all the circumstances and details, and the way my life ended.'

Reincarnation is also an integral tenet of Lamaism, the Buddhism of Tibet. Great mural paintings in Tibetan temples colourfully and fearsomely portray the relentless wheel of destiny, symbolical of the cycle of birth-death-rebirth that is the lot of all mortals. For centuries the idea of reincarnation has determined succession to the highest ecclesiastical office in Tibet, and each of the two chief prelates of Tibetan Buddhism is regarded as the *tulku* ('divine emanation') of a bodhisattva, or saviour-being: the Dalai Lama, of Avalokitesvara; and the Panchen Lama, of Amitabha.

It is believed that on the death of the chief lama of a great monastery, his spirit does not wander about looking for a body, but is immediately housed in the body of a child born at the very moment of his death. In the case of the Dalai Lama many elaborate ceremonies are undergone to determine where his successor has been born. Sometimes, before his death, the Dalai Lama intimates to his disciples where he will reappear, but in any event it becomes the duty of the college of lamas to scan the stars, consult the state oracles, read the signs in sacred lakes, and look for other omens and indications that will lead them to the true successor.

The names of all children born at the moment of the Dalai Lama's death are submitted to the assembly of abbots of all the great monasteries, and three names are finally chosen. Lots are then drawn, the auspicious signs scrutinized, and the favoured child put to certain tests. He must, for example, unerringly pick out the rosary, drinking cup, shawl and other possessions of the late Dalai Lama from among others that are placed before him, and he must also have one or more auspicious marks on his body. The little Dalai Lama is then taken away to be educated and trained for his great task by learned priests.

**Druids and Orphics**

In the western world, the Druids of ancient Britain evolved one of the earliest known philosophical systems that mitigated the desolation and hopelessness of death. In their teaching there was a complete absence of any hell or eternal punishment. No actual Druidical writings have survived, but classical authors like Julius Ceasar (d. 44 B.C.), Diodorus Siculus (d. 30 B.C.), Strabo (d. A.D. 25) and Lucan (d. A.D. 65) among others, have preserved stray traditions about them that were still current in their day. The sixth book of Caesar's *Gallic War* states that the Druids taught the doctrine of reincarnation.

According to the Druids the purpose of transmigration is to collect experiences in different spheres, to learn to distinguish between good and evil, and to learn to appreciate and choose the good. The soul does not become extinct or perish on the death of the body, nor go to any place of torment, but after living for a time with the departed ancestors it enters into another state of existence in another body in another sphere. As the Latin poet Lucan records it, 'Your teaching is that the shades of the dead do not make their way to the silent abode of Erebus (hell) or the lightless realms of Pluto (god of hell) below, but that the soul is animated elsewhere.'

The theme of reincarnation occurs in the classical world of Greece and Rome from earliest times. It underlies the great Eleusinian mysteries (*cir.* 700 B.C.), named after Eleusis, a small town lying 14 miles west of Athens. The origins of these mysteries remain obscure, but are traditionally referred back to the fifteenth century B.C., even before the Greeks had settled in the area of what is now Greece, and are said to have had their roots either in some region north of Greece, or in ancient Egypt.

Because of the stringent vows of secrecy, no one had ever divulged the actual rites. But it would appear that among the ceremonies was one depicting the *anodos*, the 'rising', or return of Persephone, daughter of Jupiter, from the dark underworld, where Pluto god of death had carried her. The central act of the Eleusinian mysteries, it is thought, was a rebirth ritual, an actual out-of-the-body experience, which gave the initiate a foretaste of the post-mortem life and of the progress of the soul thereafter.

The Orphics, another ancient mystical sect, named after the semi-legendary poet Orpheus (*c.* 650 B.C.) of Thrace, northeast of Greece, also taught the transmigration of souls, both through human and animal bodies, as well as through different supra-terrestrial regions of the universe. The Orphics spoke of the body (Gk. *soma*), as a tomb (Gk. *sema*) wherein the ethereal soul was buried. They described the soul as imprisoned in a cave, or bound to a wheel which kept eternally turning. An Orphic text speaks of deliverance from 'the sorrowful weary wheel'.

**Transmigration of Souls**

Historically the doctrine of *metempsychosis* (Greek for 'transmigration') was supposed to have been introduced to Greece by the philosopher Pherecydes (d. 544 B.C.) who taught that the soul was immortal, existing from eternity, but was trapped within the material body. After the death of the body the soul passed into another body. Good souls returned to become prophets, bards, chieftains or physicians, and those not so good returned to assume more humble roles or became animals.

His pupil, the great mathematician and philosopher Pythagoras (d. 500 B.C.) was a firm believer in the immortality of the soul, in a system of rewards and punishments according to the deserts of the individual, and in transmigration. He asserted that he had once been the herald Aethalides, son of the god Mercury, and had received from his father the gift of recollecting the transmigrations of his own soul and those of others.

The epic poet Homer relates how the Greek hero Menelaus slew the Trojan warrior Euphorbus (*c.* 1000 B.C.) and hung his shield in the temple of the goddess Juno. Five centuries later, when Pythagoras saw the shield he said he recognized it as the one he had carried as Euphorbus during his fatal encounter with Menelaus.

Pythagoras further claimed that he had lived as a prophet named Hermotimus, who was burned to death by his rivals about 200 years earlier. In other incarnations he said he had also been Pyrrhus a fisherman in Cyprus, then a prostitute in Phoenicia, a peasant in Thrace, and the wife of a shopkeeper in Lydia.

The Pythagorean doctrine was not without its critics. Foremost among them was Xenophanes (d. 480 B.C.) of Colophon, a contemporary of Pythagoras, who ridiculed the religious and mystical ideas of his day and rejected metempsychosis outright. He satirized the notion in a story he liked to tell that he once heard a dog howling and appealed to its master not to beat the animal, as he recognized in the howl the voice of a departed friend.

The physician and philosopher Empedocles (d. 432 B.C.) who also had a reputation as a soothsayer and magician, supported the Pythagorean thesis. He tells of having for 'thrice ten thousand seasons, wandered far from the blessed, being born throughout that time in the forms of all manner of mortal things and changing one baleful path of life for another. Ere now I have been a youth, a maiden, a bird, and a dumb fish in the sea'.

Plato made a more serious contribution to the subject. According to him, when the individual dies, his next incarnation is selected by himself, but how he selects is determined by his own character. If wise, he makes a wise choice, if not he is inevitably drawn into making the wrong choice.

In the concluding part of his *Republic* Plato relates the legend of Er the Pamphylian, son of Armenios, a brave man who was killed in battle and whose body was found on the twelfth day after his death and placed on the funeral pyre for cremation, when he suddenly came to life. He then told of his strange experience during those twelve days. Among other things, he said, he had beheld the colours of heaven, the axis of the world, and the destiny of individuals as decreed by the stars.

Er described how each travel-stained soul arrived in the after-death place and was told that this was where the cycle of mortal existence would start again. A person's destiny would not be allotted to him but each would have to choose for himself. Samples of lives of every animal, and of man in every condition were placed before him, mingling fame and infamy, wealth and poverty, health and disease. Past experience and knowledge would determine choice. If wise, the soul would be guided by truth and right; if unwise he would be misled by his unwisdom. The responsibility was his. The gods were guiltless in this matter. Thus the adventurous Ulysses chose a quiet retired life, for the memory of his former tumultuous existence had abated his ambitions.

It was, Er said, a wonderful sight, at once melancholy and ludicrous, to watch how each one picked his life. After they had made their choice, they drank of the waters of Lethe (Greek, 'forgetfulness') so that Mneme (Greek, 'memory') was put to sleep and they forgot all they knew. They were then despatched to their new births, this way and that, like shooting stars.

The Latin poet Ennius (d. 169 B.C.) who is credited with having introduced the theory of reincarnation to the Roman people, relates how Homer once appeared to him and told him that their bodies, separated by a thousand years, were animated by the same soul. That he, Homer, was now incarnated in Ennius.

Virgil (d. 19 B.C.) says in the *Aeneid* that the souls of the dead after a period of a thousand years are summoned to appear before the river Lethe to forget their former lives so that they are once more willing to revisit the vaulted realms of earth in living bodies.

Another Roman poet Ovid (d. A.D. 17) was convinced that he had taken part in the Trojan War many centuries before. In his *Metamorphosis* he writes that the souls of those who are departed leave their former abode to inhabit new dwellings, and in this manner they pass from tenement to tenement.

Lastly, Apollonius of Tyana (d. A.D. 98) Pythagorean philosopher, fabled wonder-worker and friend of the emperors Vespasian, Titus and Nerva, asserted that he remembered his own previous lives as a baker in Susa, an Egyptian ship's pilot, a Persian princess, and a beggar in Corinth.

### Jewish Theology and Reincarnation

The Jewish position with regard to reincarnation seems to have varied at different times, although some students claim that references in the Hebrew writings suggesting a belief in this doctrine are very abundant.

In the Book of Job, Eliphaz the Temanite says, 'They that plow iniquity, and sow wickedness, reap the same' (Job 4.8), the implication here allegedly being that Job was suffering for the sins of his former life.

In the Psalms we have the verse, 'Thou turnest man to destruction; and sayest, Return, ye children of men' (Ps. 90.3). In Malachi there is the verse reading: 'Behold, I will send you Elijah the prophet before the coming of the great and dreadful day of the Lord' (Mal. 4.5).

In the apocryphal *Wisdom of Solomon* we read: 'As a child I was born to excellence, and a noble soul fell to my lot; or rather, I myself was noble, and I entered into an unblemished body' (8. 19-20).

Philo Judaeus (d. A.D.50) Jewish philosopher of Alexandria, spoke of the soul's repeated 'expatriations' from heaven until it was absolved from all earthly allurements.

The Jewish historian Josephus (d. A.D.101) wrote, 'All pure and holy spirits live on in heavenly places, and in course of time they are again sent down to inhabit righteous bodies.' Indeed, Josephus refers to reincarnation as being commonly accepted among the Jews of his time. He states that there were three major Jewish philosophical schools in his day: the Sadducees, the Pharisees, and the Essenes.

The Sadducees did not believe in the immortality of the soul, and held that the soul, if it existed, died with the body. The Pharisees believed in the pre-existence and immortality of the soul, and also that the soul had the power to live again and again in corporeal form in successive lives. The Essenes also taught reincarnation. They held that although the body is corruptible, the soul, which temporarily resides in it, is immortal, and continues to exist for ever. Souls inhabit bodies as prisoners a prison, and yearn to be free. But because of the lure of carnal desires they are drawn-repeatedly to the material sphere until in time they learn the truth and are liberated for ever.

There are only hints of reincarnation in the talmudic writings. On the other hand the Karaites (*c.* A.D.800), a sect which rejected the Talmud, emphatically upheld the doctrine of rebirth. The teaching was first systematically set forth in the *Bahir* (*c.* 1180), an obscure hermetic treatise, which spoke of reincarnation as *gilgul* (Hebrew, 'circuit' or 'rotation'), and stated that every soul must go through the experience of gilgul.

Similarly, the Zohar (*c.* 1300), the chief text of the medieval

Jewish mystical system known as the Kabalah, frequently alludes to the subject of the soul's return. It states that the soul of Eve was successively reincarnated in Sarah, in the Shunamite, and in the widow of Zarephath; that of Abel was reborn in Moses; that of Jacob in Mordecai; of Laban in Nabal; of Tamar in Ruth; of Aaron in Eli and Ezra; of Rahab in Hannah; and of Phinehas in Elijah.

According to the Zohar, all souls are subject to the trials of transmigration, and men do not realize how many mysterious transformations they must undergo. Ultimately all souls will enter the Absolute, but to accomplish this they must first develop every perfection, the seeds of which are planted in them. If they have not succeeded in one life, they must start another, and a third. One text states that a wicked soul after three chances becomes a *dibbuk* or evil spirit. Other Kabalists state that there is no limit to the number of chances a soul is given, and it goes on and on until in the end it has acquired the condition that fits it for its reunion with God.

In spite of the evidence in the Kabalah, many Hebrew authorities deny that reincarnation plays any significant part in the Jewish faith.

**Gnosticism and Neoplatonism**

Whether the doctrine was accepted among the early Christians is likewise disputed, although advocates maintain that the Gospels do provide evidence that reincarnation was implicit in certain statements made by Christ, and that it also formed part of the teachings of the early church fathers. We shall consider this evidence in a later chapter.

Most of the major mystical schools that flourished during the early Christian era, such as the Gnostics, Neoplatonists and Hermetics, took reincarnation for granted.

The leading Gnostic teachers were: Basilides (d. A.D. 130) and Carpocrates (d. 135), both of Alexandria; Marcion (d. 160) of Sinope on the shores of the Black Sea; and Valentinus (d. 165) also of Alexandria. Their teachings were a mixture of Zoroastrian dualism and Buddhist transmigrationism, with a liberal sprinkling of Phrygian sensuality sometimes added.

This latter element is most blatantly exemplified in the teachings of Carpocrates, who said that reincarnation was necessary for *gnosis* (Gk. 'enlightenment') and salvation. It is essential that souls in their successive incarnations have as many and as varied experiences as possible, both pleasurable and painful, virtuous and evil, glorious and sordid. Men and women are given physical bodies that they might savour sensual pleasure in all its variations to the full, and they should therefore not neglect the opportunities provided.

Among the Neoplatonists, sometimes referred to as the Philalethians or 'lovers of truth', the philosopher Plotinus (d. A.D.270) believed that the soul rises from the body at death carrying with it the total experience of what it has been and suffered. He wrote: 'The soul that has sinned expiates its sins in the darkness of the infernal regions and afterwards passes into the receptacle of a new body, to undergo fresh trials to gain a clear knowledge of right and wrong. This is a dogma recognized throughout antiquity.'

The Roman emperor Julian the Apostate (d. A.D.363) who came under the influence of Neoplatonism, claimed to have been Alexander the Great in a previous life.

Hermeticism (*c.* A.D.150-400), a school of esoteric knowledge named after Hermes Trismegistus, the Greek title of the Egyptian god Thoth, also accepts transmigration. Thus, one of the hermetic manuscripts, *The Divine Pymander* (*c.* A.D.150) states, 'That which has its operation in time and space is subject, like all nature, to increase and decrease, generation and corruption, and unless time and space are transcended the progress of man must resolve itself into a never-ending series of revolutions of the wheel of birth and death, from which there can be no ultimate escape.' According to this document, it is only when man becomes truly self-aware, and realizes his inherent immortality separate from the laws of natural birth, that he enters upon his supernatural regeneration.

### The Islamic View

In Islam transmigration is known as *tanasukh*, though it is generally treated as being alien to the teachings of the Prophet. Arab and Persian theologians sometimes discussed the possibility of rebirth as a likely consequence of an evil or unfulfilled life. The idea of tanasukh is more widespread among Moslems in India, perhaps because of Hindu influence. The following are among the verses in the Koran quoted in support of it.

> 'How can you make denial of Allah, who made you live again when you died, will make you dead again, and then alive again, until you finally return to him' (Koran 2.28). 'We said to him who broke the sabbath, Be you apes, despised and hated' (Koran, 2.65). 'Worse is he whom Allah has cursed and brought his wrath upon, and whom he has turned into apes and swine' (Koran, 5.60). 'Allah has caused you to grow as a growth from earth, and afterwards he makes you return thereto, and he will bring you forth again' (Koran, 71, 17-18).

Several of the celebrated Persian sufi poets, notably Jalaluddin Rumi (d. 1273), Saadi (d. 1291), and Hafiz (d. 1390) implied in their verses the possibility of the soul's return to the material plane. Rumi was more explicit than most. He wrote:

> Like grass I have grown over and over again. I passed out of mineral form and lived as a plant. From plant I was lifted up to be an animal. Then I put away the animal form and took on human shape. Why should I fear that if I died I shall be lost? For passing human form I shall attain the flowing locks and shining wings of angels. And then I shall become what no mind ever conceived. O let me cease to exist! For non-existence only means that I shall return to Him.

The Druse religion, practised by people living mostly in the Lebanon and Syria, is a syncretic and heretical offshoot of Islam, founded in the eleventh century by the Fatimid caliph al-Hakim, who mysteriously vanished in 1021, and was believed to have reappeared again and again in the different illustrious leaders of the sect.

Reincarnation is a fundamental Druse tenet. By their devotion to the truth, they say, souls are raised to excellence, and conversely, by their neglect of it are degraded in their next rebirth. The Druses believe that on his death a person's soul passes immediately into the body of a baby born at the same instant, there being no interval between death and rebirth (Stevenson, 1974, p.273).

## Christianity and Reincarnation

Although mainstream Christianity denied reincarnation, there were a number of heretical sects in the middle ages that did perpetuate the doctrine. These sects are often classed together as Cathars, 'pure', a term originally applied by St Augustine (d. 430) to the Manichaeans (above). The Cathars were dualistic in their theology and generally ascetic in practice.

They included the Paulicans of Thrace (tenth century); the Bogomils of Bulgaria (eleventh century), one of whose leaders, John Italus, made metempsychosis the focal point of his teaching; the Patarenes of the Balkans and northern Italy (twelfth century); and the Albigensians of southern France (thirteenth century).

Linked with the Cathars were the Knights Templars (thirteenth and fourteenth centuries), a Christian military order founded to protect pilgrims visiting the holy land. The Templars in turn are thought to have been influenced by the Druses and Saracens. Indeed one of the main charges levelled against the Templars by the Inquisition was that they were infected with the Cathar heresy and 'Moorish practices'.

Also sympathetic to the Cathar ideology were the troubadours, the travelling minstrels who wandered around Europe between the eleventh and thirteenth centuries, and were especially prominent in Provence and Languedoc. Among the great heroes whose exploits they celebrated in their mystical songs were King Arthur and his knights, and Charlemagne and his paladins. At the same time many of the troubadours popularized the Cathar teachings in their ballads, including the notion that each person had to pass through a cycle of imprisonment in the flesh, perhaps even twelve times or more, before being finally liberated.

The principal fortress and sacred place of the Cathars (Albigensians) was situated on Montségur in the Pyrenees, near Toulouse, and here some 200 of the faithful, men and women, were burned to death by the Inquisition. This event took place in 1244 and marked the end of the Albigensians as a sect, although in various ways their influence continued for centuries after.

Many of the European occult schools, medieval and modern, have also upheld the premiss of the soul's immortality and its continuing return to earth in order to perfect its destiny. Chief among these schools are the Illuminati (fifteenth century), the

Alchemists (thirteenth to seventeenth centuries), the Rosicrucians (sixteen and seventeenth centuries), the Martinists (eighteenth century), the Spiritualists and Theosophists (nineteenth and twentieth centuries).

The theory was elaborately worked out, on the analogy of their laboratory practice, by the alchemists, who compared the search for the philosopher's stone with man's search for his own soul, hidden in dross, which had to be purified in the furnace of suffering and be raised to high estate. The repeated purifications and sublimations, the constant heating in the crucible, were symbolic of the dissolution of the flesh and the resurrection of of the spirit, and of the soul's experiences both in the present life and in other lives on earth.

The leading theorists of the alchemical system who supported reincarnation were Raymond Lully (d. 1315) Catalan scholar, Paracelsus (d. 1541) Swiss-German physician, Robert Fludd (d. 1637) English physician, and Thomas Vaughan (d. 1666) Welsh mystic. The naturalist, alchemist, philosopher and physician, Franz Mercurius van Helmont (d. 1699) set forth 200 queries and answers relating to the doctrine of the return of souls based largely on Kabalist teachings.

**Spiritualism and Theosophy**

The modern spiritualist movement dates from 1848, when the Fox sisters, Kate and Margaret, heard the alleged spirit knockings in their home in Hydesville, Rochester, New York State. Within a decade spiritualism had become a world-wide movement.

Generally speaking, spiritualists did not sponsor the idea of reincarnation. The conspicuous exception was Allan Kardec (d. 1869) pseudonym of Hippolyte Rivail, French author of *The Book of Spirits* and other works on spiritism, a term he preferred to spiritualism. The main tenet of spiritism is that the spiritual progress of the individual is attained as a result of a series of incarnations. The book is based on trance communications received through Mlle Celina Bequet, a professional medium. This lady's mediumship was developed by the 'mesmerist' Monsieur Roustan, who believed in the plurality of individual lives in successive bodies, and this probably influenced the kind of messages that came through. Kardec's brand of spiritism not only became fashionable in France, but also took root in Brazil where it had an enormous following, and where there are at present over 300 spiritist societies.

In the vanguard of the modern reincarnationist revival, as indeed of most other forms of modern occultism, was the Theosophical Society. It was founded in 1875 by Madame Helena Petrovna Blavatsky (d. 1891), who professed to be a reincarnation of Pythagoras (d. 500 B.C.). She also claimed to remember vividly the details of her past life as Paracelsus (d. 1541).

Her colleague, and co-founder of the Theosophical Society, Col. Henry Steele Olcott, was an American lawyer who had served in the Federal forces during the civil war. Olcott stated that he had previously lived as a prince in Atlantis, and then as Odysseus (Ulysses), as well as several other illustrious personages of the past.

Blavatsky's disciple, Annie Besant (d. 1933), although a materialist and agnostic to begin with, once she had met Blavatsky could not be restrained from taking the 'mad step' as G.B. Shaw called it, of joining the mystical band. She became a staunch supporter of reincarnation and claimed that she herself in her first embodiment lived on the moon in 600,000 B.C.. Her other lives included Hypatia (d. A.D.415) female neoplatonist martyr who was torn to pieces by a mob in Alexandria. She had also been the Italian rebel thinker Giordano Bruno (d. 1600), himself a believer in transmigration, who was burned at the stake in Rome. Four years before being born in her current incarnation Annie Besant had died as a brahmin pundit in the Himalayas.

The English landscape painter, John Varley (d. 1933) joined the Theosophical Society, and under the inspiration of its teachings drew curious coloured illustrations of human auras and emotions and thus gave modern art a new orientation, creating an interest in the distortion of form, in abstract painting, and in clairvoyant art (Nethercot, 1963, p.90).

Charles Webster Leadbeater (d. 1934) the theosophist, in his book *The Soul's Growth Through Reincarnation*, traced Varley's past lives, 17 in all, ten as a man and seven as a woman, starting as an entity named Erato, who lived in 19,245 B.C. in Chaldea. At different times, according to Leadbeater, Varley had been a Chinese, European, Indian, Japanese, Eskimo, South American,

Egyptian, as well as an inhabitant of the submerged continent of Atlantis. The average period between incarnations, he said, was 1264 years.

Among the early offshoots of the Theosophical Society were the Hermetic Society and the Anthroposophical Society.

The Hermetic Society, an amalgam of theosophy, gnosticism and Kabalism, was founded in 1884 by Anna Kingsford (d. 1888) and her admirer, amanuensis and biographer, Edward Maitland. Anna Kingsford, who was originally a theosophist and had converted Annie Besant to vegetarianism, believed that she was the reincarnation of the Virgin Mary. Her friend Maitland claimed to be the reincarnation of St John the Divine.

The Anthroposophisical Society was founded in 1913 by Rudolf Steiner (d. 1925) also a former member of the Theosophical Society. Steiner stated that human evolution began in the antediluvian civilizations of Lemuria and Atlantis, and that in the course of its progress to enlightenment the human soul after successive lives on earth, will proceed to the planetary spheres, and thence to the sun where it will arrive at a true understanding of itself. From there it will go on to the stars and so on until it attains to a relationship with the whole spiritual world (Shepherd, 1954).

The English magician Aleister Crowley (d. 1947) wrote a book on the technique of remembering past lives by following the path of memory in reverse. He himself claimed to remember many of his past incarnations, among them the following. A Cretan princess named Aia (*c.* 2500 B.C.) related to King Minos. A Theban priest of the 26th dynasty of ancient Egypt named Ankh-af-na-Khonsu (d. 666 B.C.), whose name signifies, 'His life is in Khonsu,' Khonsu being the moon deity of Thebes. The Chinese sage Ko Hsuen (d. 470 B.C.) a disciple of the great Lao Tzu. A Roman named Marius Aquila (d. A.D. 370) who lived in the time of Julian the Apostate. Khaled Khan (d. A.D. 642) who defeated the Christians at the battle of Damascus. An adept or occult master who lived in Central Europe in about A.D. 890. The notorious Borgia pope, Alexander VI (d. 1503). Edward Kelly (d. 1597) the skryer of the famous Welsh mystic and occultist John Dee. Count Alessandro di Cagliostro (d. 1795) alchemist and necromancer. Eliphas Lévi (d. 1875) French mage who died in the year Crowley was born.

Scores of poets, novelists, philosophers and thinkers of the Western world have considered reincarnation to be the most reasonable and acceptable explanation for some of the problems of life. A few representative individuals are quoted below.

David Hume (d. 1776) Scottish philosopher and sceptic in religion, wrote that assuming the soul exists, then metempsychosis is the only system that 'philosophy can hearken to'.

Charles de Bonnet (d. 1793) Swiss naturalist, philosopher and psychologist was convinced of the soul's immortality and rebirth.

Napoleon (d. 1821) several times asserted that he was the reincarnation of Charlemagne (d. 814), king of the Franks and Roman emperor.

Arthur Schopenhauer (d. 1860) regarded it as an incredible delusion of the Western world that man's present birth was his first entrance into life. In his view, 'When we die we throw off our personality like a worn-out garment, and rejoice because we are about to receive a new and better one.'

Henry David Thoreau (d. 1862) author of *Walden*, wrote, 'Methinks the hawk that soars so loftily and circles so steadily and apparently without effort, has earned this power by faithfully creeping on the ground as a reptile in a former state of existence.' Elsewhere he says, 'It is unavoidable, the idea of transmigration; not merely a fancy of the poets, but an instinct of the race.' And again, in his *Journals* we read, 'I have lived in Judea eighteen hundred years ago... I sauntered in old heroic times amid the ruins of chariots and heroes... I was a shepherd in Assyria.'

Thomas Henry Huxley (d. 1895) in his *Evolution and Ethics* discerned a parallel between the concepts of heredity and of reincarnation; he found that the qualities we inherit from our parents and progenitors have some relationship to the idea of transmigration. What we call character, the Indian philosophers called karma. In his view, 'None but very hasty thinkers will reject reincarnation on the ground of inherent absurdity.'

Count Leo Tolstoy (d. 1910) greatest of the Russian novelists wrote, 'Our whole life is a dream. As we live through thousands of dreams in our present life, so is our present life only one of thousands of such lives we enter from the more real life, the life of God, and then return to after death. I believe it. I know it. I see it without a doubt'.

John Masefield (d. 1976) English poet and novelist, in his poem, 'A Creed', says that when a person dies his old soul returns again to earth, born of another mother, and disguised in new flesh, and then 'takes the roads again'.

# 3
# Some Modern Examples

Historically, the theory of reincarnation can be traced back thousands of years. Serious investigation of case histories, on the other hand, is less than a century old. The cases so studied may be divided into two broad categories. The first relates predominantly to the eastern hemisphere, where the belief is widely prevalent, and where the subject is often young and claims to have conscious remembrance usually of his immediate past life. The second relates to the western hemisphere, where the belief is not commonly held, and where the subject is usually an adult who is able to remember his past, often going back many centuries, generally only under hypnosis.

Hundreds of cases of both categories have been investigated, and here it is possible to recount briefly, and in some instances analyse, only a sampling of the more important ones, a few of which have become classics of their kind.

One of the most interesting cases dating from the last century, is recorded by the English statesman, traveller, occultist, and one-time special correspondent of *The Times*, Laurence Oliphant (d. 1888). While in the Lebanon he noted that reincarnation was one of the fundamental teachings of the Druses. In his book entitled *The Land of Gilead, with Excursions in the Lebanon* (1880) Oliphant tells the story of a five-year-old child, born in Jebel el A'ala to very poor parents, who complained that in a previous life he had been a wealthy man in Damascus, and that on the latter's death he had been born again in another place, but had lived only six months, to be born once more into his present impoverished family.

The boy insisted that he be taken to Damascus, and on the

way showed a remarkable knowledge of the places they passed through, correctly naming them. At Damascus he went unaided through the streets until he reached the house of his earlier life, and on being admitted called the woman of the house by her name, told her he had been her husband, and asked about the welfare of his children, relations and friends.

Hearing about this, the Druses of the place began to question the child more closely, and he was able to give them an accurate account of his life among them. He also came up with many small details about himself, about his former friends, neighbours and acquaintances, including even their business affairs. He said that a certain weaver still owed him a sum of money, and the man, being produced, acknowledged the debt, but pleaded his inability to pay because of his poverty. These and many other facts were all shown to be true.

The boy then asked his 'wife' whether she had found a certain sum of money he had concealed in the cellar of their house, and when she said she had not, he went, accompanied by witnesses, without the slightest hesitation, down to the cellar, dug up the money and counted it before them. It was the exact sum he had indicated.

**Marie Mayo**

Another well-known case comes from the files of one of the earliest investigators to try age regression through hypnosis, the French psychical researcher Col. Eugène Albert de Rochas (d. 1914). Among his subjects was a certain Mlle Marie Mayo, the daughter of a French engineer, who while in hypnotic trance was taken through childhood and infancy back to her former life as Lina, the young daughter of a Brittany fisherman. At the age of twenty she had married a fisherman named Yvon (she did not recall his family name), and bore him a child who died at the age of two. When her husband was drowned in a shipwreck, she threw herself in a fit of despair from the top of a cliff into the sea, where her body was eaten by fishes. During her recital of this dramatic incident Marie passed through the convulsions of drowning.

In an incarnation before that, Marie had lived as a man named Charles Mauville, who was employed as a clerk in a ministerial office in Paris in the reign of Louis XVIII. This man was very wicked, a murderer, who died at the age of fifty. Still earlier she had been Madeleine de Saint-Marc, whose husband was attached to the French court.

Yet the value of this French pioneer's work was cast in serious doubt by another claim he made. According to Col. Rochas he was able, by means of longitudinal passes, to take his subjects back into the past. But he also claimed that by transverse passes some of his subjects could be made to go forward into the lives they would live in their future incarnations. The rigid determinism implicit in this claim was repudiated by most other psychical researchers of the day, and brought the theory of reincarnation into ridicule in many circles.

**Shanti Devi**

In 1933, a seven-year old girl, Shanti Devi, born in 1926 in Delhi, insisted that she had lived before in the town of Muttra (Mathura), about 100 miles away. Then, she claimed, she had been called Ludgi, who was born in 1902, had been married and had three children, but had died in giving birth to her third child. She was reborn in her present incarnation about a year after her previous death.

When in 1935 a man named Shri Lal visited their house on business, the girl gave a cry of surprise, declaring that he was her husband's cousin. The visitor confirmed that he did indeed come from Muttra and had a cousin whose wife Ludgi had died in childbirth ten years earlier.

Subsequently, Ludgi's husband, Kedar Nath Chaubey, was brought to the house without Shanti being informed beforehand, and on seeing him she immediately ran forward, addressing him as she would her husband. The girl was then taken to Muttra where she recognized her two elder children, but not the child at whose birth she had died. She also identified relatives, friends and acquaintances of her former embodiment, conversed with many people who knew the Kedar Nath household, and amazed everyone with her detailed knowledge of past events. She went about the town, correctly pointing out the various places which had been known to Ludgi, showing perfect familiarity with the neighbourhood.

Investigators who later examined the data, found that the case, as presented by the experts of the time, had a number of unsatisfactory features. It lacked the necessary safeguards against misinterpretation. Alternative hypotheses had not been carefully considered, and other possible explanations for the facts not put forward. For instance, it came to light that Kedar Nath, the widower, often visited Delhi and bought sweetmeats from a shop within a few yards of Shanti's house.

There seemed to be a tendency among the early workers in the field to resist or soft-pedal any evidence that might weaken their case. It is also possible that the statements attributed to Shanti were unwittingly suggested to her by her relations and outsiders interested in establishing the case for reincarnation, which is one of the bulwarks of Hindu belief. Shanti's grand-uncle, Professor Kishen Chand, took over the investigation from the time that Shanti was a mere eight years of age, and may have unconsciously directed his enquiries along lines that favoured the rebirth idea.

When in 1958, nearly a quarter of a century later, a reporter interviewed Shanti Devi, who was then working as a government employee in New Delhi, she refused to give any further information saying, 'I do not want to open that closed door again' (Ebon, 1970, p.47).

Among those who investigated her case at the time were a schoolmaster, a nationalist leader, a well-known lawyer, and the editor of an Indian newspaper. The manner of investigation, both by Indians and outsiders, was by and large amateurish and wide-eyed, and tending to sensationalism. Dr Ian Stevenson, a most careful investigator, described the case in 1960, but by this time most of the data could only have been examined at second or third remove.

The case of Shanti Devi, had it occurred today, would have been subjected to a much greater degree of scientific treatment from an Indian team. Some of the best known investigators today are Indian scholars, who have examined in scrupulous detail the evidence in scores of alleged cases of reincarnation and written authoritative accounts of them, and many have achieved international eminence in the field. Notable among them are Professor Hemendra N. Banerjee, director of the department of parapsychology in Rajasthan University, Jaipur; Professor B.L. Atreya, professor of philosophy in Banaras University; Professor P. Pal of Itachuna College, West Bengal;

and Dr Jamuna Prasad, deputy director of education, Uttar Pradesh.

**Edgar Cayce**

Perhaps the most famous reincarnationist of this century was the American psychic and clairvoyant, Edgar Cayce (1877-1945), born near Hopkinsville, Kentucky. From early childhood Cayce was dreamy and withdrawn. He had imaginary playmates and once talked to an angel. He had the so-called gift of second sight, heard voices, and saw and spoke to 'visions', his dead grandfather among them.

Once, at the age of nine, after being reprimanded by an impatient uncle because he could not spell, he fell off the chair on which he was sitting and lay on the floor in a coma. A voice told him that if he slept a little he would be helped. He slept for fifteen minutes with the spelling book under his pillow and awoke to find that he knew every lesson in the book. At the age of sixteen he received an injury to the spine, was brought home and put to bed and again went into a coma. Then, quite suddenly, in a clear and steady voice, he prescribed a herbal cure. The attending physician decided to give this unorthodox remedy a try, with spectacular results. The boy awoke the next day fresh and restored to health. He remembered nothing of what he had said, and when questioned it was found that he had never heard of most of the plants he had named.

At the age of twenty-four Cayce contracted a throat ailment, resulting in a loss of voice, which refused to respond to ordinary medical treatment. In desperation he sought the help of an amateur hypnotist, Al Layne. Under hypnosis Cayce once more prescribed a cure for himself, which worked with equal success. When word of his extraordinary ability spread, neighbours and friends begged him to prescribe for them.

A group of physicians from Hopkinsville and the adjacent areas took advantage of his talent and sought his help in the diagnosis of their patients. One of them, Dr Wesley Ketchum, made out a report on the Cayce method to a medical research organization in Boston, and in October 1910 *The New York Times* carried a story about him. The result was that people from all over the country wrote asking for help in their physical ailments.

Cayce was apparently able to see the coloured aura around a

person's head and shoulders, and from the colour and condition of the aura could determine the patient's character and state of health. But his usual procedure was to go into a trance. He would lie on his back, hands folded across his chest, and start breathing deeply. The fluttering of his eyelids was a signal for the 'conductor', who was usually his wife Gertrude, or his father Leslie, to close his eyes and start asking questions. Because of this method he came to be known as 'the sleeping prophet'.

The remedies he prescribed included massage, poultices, electric treatment, special diets, spinal manipulation, herbs, and a wide variety of curious substances like 'peach-tree packs', 'bamboo ash', 'bedbug juice' and 'oil of smoke'. The presence of the patient was not necessary, as he could 'see the body' and prescribe for people if they just sent him particulars of their ailments by post.

As his work increased a stenographer was engaged to take down what he said. On awaking he never remembered anything. It was thought that during his self-induced slumber he was literally being used as a mouthpiece by the spirits of dead medical specialists, but Cayce was not a 'spiritualist' and had no 'guides' or 'controls'.

In 1923 a certain Arthur Lammers, who had made a thorough study of psychic phenomena and eastern religions, invited Cayce to Dayton, Ohio, paying for the prophet's expenses all the way from Selma, Alabama. On 10 August, in a hotel room with a stenographer present, Cayce, at Lammer's request, put himself into hypnotic sleep. While Cayce was thus entranced Lammers 'bombarded' him with questions (Langley, 1967, p.12).

Unfortunately we are not told much about the nature of the interrogation, but it would be interesting to know whether leading questions were put to him or suggestions implanted in his subconscious mind. In any event the session marked a turning point in Cayce's career, for when the stenographer read back the transcript of the session, he was horrified to discover that his psychic voice had insisted on the reality of reincarnation. Lammers, it is said, was jubilant.

The reason for Cayce's sense of outrage was that he was a devout fundamentalist Christian, a life-long Sunday School teacher, who had read the Bible from cover to cover every year for forty years, and he found the idea of reincarnation alien and repulsive to his sentiments and contrary to his religious upbringing. But despite what he believed to be the sacrilegious character of his utterances, he allowed Lammers to continue questioning him, after the first shock was over.

The floodgates had been opened, for the deep instinct that Cayce obviously had for the occult was from now on to find full and uninhibited expression. On 11 October 1923, just two months after the initial session with Lammers, Cayce made his first trance pronouncement about a subject's previous incarnation: 'Third appearance in this plane. He was once a monk'. From that day on, till his death in January 1945, a period of twenty-one years, Cayce gave approximately 2500 'life readings', dealing with past lives on earth, explained in terms of 'karmic patterns'. In these life readings Cayce would trace a person's ailments or abnormalities, if any, including phobias, marriage difficulties, work dissatisfaction, unsocial behaviour, back to acts committed by the 'entity', as the subject was called, in a previous life in medieval Europe, pre-Columbian America, the Middle East, Rome, Greece or Atlantis. Almost 50 per cent of his patients apparently had incarnations in Atlantis.

Whenever he was asked for a cure, he began to look for the solution to the patient's problems in a past life. From now on the conductor presumed reincarnation in every instance, and put this to Cayce without equivocation. She would give the sleeping healer the name, date and place of birth of the patient, and then proceed to ask for particulars of 'the former appearances in the earth's plane', with names, times and places, and an account of what has helped or hindered development of the entity. Two examples of Cayce life readings will suffice.

A young girl named Irene McGinley, aged seventeen, bedridden with cancer of the femur, was informed that she had been the daughter of a wealthy and influential Roman official in the time of the emperor Nero. Another girl attached to the household at the time was a secret Christian, in love with a man whom Irene herself also favoured. To get rid of her rival Irene had betrayed the girl to the Roman authorities, and she was torn to death by wild beasts in the ampitheatre. The broken-hearted lover died of grief. Because of this, in her present life Irene was being pitied and scorned for her inability to participate in any activity that required the full use of her physical body.

The life reading of a fourteen year old boy named David Greenwood included the following pre-incarnations. He had lived as a man named Neil, who was a kind of Master of the Robes at the French court during the reigns of Louis XIII and XIV; as a tradesman named Colval in Greece; as a court physician in Persia named Abiel during the time of Alexander's invasion; as a religious leader named Isois in ancient Egypt (*c.* 10,000 B.C.) who came to be worshipped as a minor deity after his death, and as a prince of Atlantis named Amiaie-Oulieb, heir-apparent to the throne, who died by drowning.

Edgar Cayce himself was said to have been born in an earlier incarnation in 1742 as John Bainbridge. Of Cornish stock he had left England for America, landing in Chesapeake Bay, significantly near Virginia Beach, where the headquarters of the present organization dedicated to the study of Cayce's work was to be established some two centuries later. A life of adventure took Bainbridge from the Canadian border to Florida, and involved him in skirmishes with Indian tribes. He died while helping a group of men, women and children to escape on a raft down the Ohio river.

Earlier still Cayce had been a priest named Ra-Ta, who accompanied his people from the Carpathian region during their conquest of Egypt about 10,500 B.C. In Egypt, Ra-Ta set about organizing their religious practices. It was at this period too that refugees from doomed Atlantis were crowding into Egypt. Ra-Ta took part in a native rebellion and was exiled to what is now Abyssinia, but was recalled after nine years to help in the material and spiritual regeneration of the country (Cayce, 1968, p.150).

Cayce had always been interested in the occult. He had once worked as an assistant in a bookshop, and was known to be a voracious reader who devoured a vast quantity of books on miscellaneous subjects. His reading interests from an early age had embraced Biblical stories, ancient history, ancient mythology, the antediluvian legends, the lost continents of Lemuria, Mu and Atlantis, the land of Oz (said to have been in ancient Peru), primitive healing, faith-healing, osteopathy, herbal remedies, homeopathy, the Essenes, theosophy, out-of-the-body travel, dream interpretation, the time barrier, extrasensory perception, UFOs, spiritualism, the ouija board, dowsing, prophecy, astrology, genetics, the races of mankind, the destiny of nations, the end of the world, the millennium.

Some of this background no doubt came to the surface in his healing trances. Henceforth, every aspect of esotericism known to him was incorporated into the life readings and his prophetic utterances. From being hostile to the doctrine of reincarnation, he made it an integral part of his work and message. The fundamentalist Christian now believed that the spirit of Christ manifested on earth twenty-nine times before the coming of Jesus, incarnating as a major figure within the religious movements in other parts of the world (Goodman, 1977, p.64). Jesus himself was an advanced adept who had worked out all his karma.

It has been suggested that Cayce may have unconsciously fallen victim to his own preoccupation with the occult. A simple and kindly soul he himself is above suspicion. Those who knew him personally vouched for his personal integrity. One of the earliest and most sympathetic biographies of Cayce, *There is a River*, was written by his friend, an American Catholic named Thomas Sugrue. From 1937 Sugrue had been confined to a wheelchair, with a rare form of arthritis. He died in 1953. That the book went into thirteen printings, totalling 1,050,000 copies, indicates the extent of popular interest in Cayce and his mission.

The ARE, or Association for Research and Enlightenment, with headquarters at Virginia Beach, Virginia, is a memorial to Cayce's work. It is dedicated to the study and analysis of his 15,000 or so stenographic transcripts dating from 1932, amounting to 14 million words on 90,000 typewritten pages. The material, indexed on over 200,000 cards, is enough to fill 200 volumes. The ARE has some 800 loosely affiliated study units.

While many accounts of Cayce tend to treat him as a twentieth-century Hippocrates or Nostradamus, his critics point out that he was often wrong in his prophecies, and that his alleged healings were seldom substantiated by independent medical opinion. What percentage of success he had with his cures was long debated and remains unsettled. In one conspicuous case at least, where expert confirmation might have helped to silence his critics, it was not forthcoming. Cayce had given a medical reading for the small daughter of Dr Joseph B. Rhine, the famous parapsychologist of Duke University, but it proved to be a misdiagnosis and did not fit the facts (Gardner, 1957, p.219).

The accuracy of his predictions is equally in dispute, both as to dates and their fulfilment. Often his utterances were too ambiguous and obscure. His accounts of past lives were so vague as to be beyond proving. Dr Ian Stevenson, who has studied hundreds of reincarnation claims, states that in the 'vast majority of cases' it is not possible to establish the existence of the person mentioned by Cayce as having been in the past the person for whom the reading was given (Ebon, 1970, p.11). In fact, few of his 2500 life readings present any data that offer scope for verification. They are all historically valueless. Finally, it is said, his penchant for putting so many of his entities back into Atlantis imposes a great strain on belief, and a fair percentage of his patients simply ignored his readings.

**Bridey Murphy**

Perhaps the best known of all cases of alleged reincarnation was that of Bridey Murphy, reported in a best-selling book written by a prosperous young businessman and amateur hypnotist of Pueblo, Colorado, named Morey Bernstein. He had become quite skilled in the practice of hypnosis, and had helped a number of people to overcome mild conditions of psychosomatic origin, such as migraine, smoking, shyness, stammering and insomnia. For amusement he used to practice a kind of cocktail party hypnotism at various country-club functions. Among his subjects was Virginia Tighe, a young Colorado housewife and mother of two children. She appears in Bernstein's book under the pseudonym of Ruth Simmons, which at the time was designed to protect her identity.

In 1950 Bernstein had been given copies of Thomas Sugrue's biography of Edgar Cayce, *There is a River*, and Gina Cerminara's *Many Mansions*, both of which dealt with age regression under hypnosis and the possibility of tapping memories of a past life. As a hypnotist Bernstein had never tried this himself. He did not accept the doctrine of reincarnation, and refused to believe in the genuineness of the experiments. He accordingly decided to go to the Cayce headquarters at Virginia Beach and inspect the original documents, and also interrogate the people who had had first-hand experience with the readings. His express intention was to expose Cayce as a fraud (Langley, 1967, p.217).

He returned to Pueblo a more thoughtful man, and decided to give the age-regression technique a trial. He chose Mrs Virginia Tighe as a likely subject. Under hypnosis he guided her back to her adolescence, her childhood, her infancy, and then to the first few moments after birth. He then had to take what he called 'the big step', making her go back to a period before her present life, into an earlier incarnation.

During the six sessions, which were recorded on tape in 1952, Virginia Tighe began talking in an Irish brogue, relating her past life as an Irish girl named Bridey Murphy, born in County Cork, Ireland, in 1798, of her barrister father Duncan and her mother Kathleen. She gave a wealth of data covering this early life, including details of places, events, household furniture, domestic articles, kitchen utensils, food, coinage, farming, crops, and books, much of it unknown to contemporary Americans and Irishmen, but, it was assumed, familiar to the Irish at the time of her past life. Bridey was married at twenty to a law clerk named Sean Brian McCarthy and died childless in Belfast at the age of sixty-six as a result of a fall down some steps. After her bodily death she existed in the spirit world, to be reborn in 1922 as Ruth Simmons.

Bernstein's book, recounting his experiment, was published in 1956 under the title of *The Search for Bridey Murphy*.

William Barker, a journalist, whose articles in the *Denver Post* in 1954 had aroused public interest in the experiments even before the book appeared, went to Ireland to do a little detective work. But he was unable to find any positive information about anyone named Bridey Murphy who had lived in the place mentioned, or about anyone else mentioned in the book. A number of individuals sponsored by newspapers, publishers and other organizations, also made an intensive search for corroborative details about Bridey Murphy and for evidence of her existence, but without success. No firm evidence of any value seemed to be forthcoming from Ireland.

However, an attempt was made to look into the background of Mrs. Virginia Tighe herself, and it was then that a series of interesting facts allegedly came to light. The *Chicago American* found several parallels between Virginia's actual childhood and the Bridey Murphy memories, and other investigators soon added further clues.

Virginia was born in 1922 in a white frame house in Madison, Wisconsin, exactly like the house described by Bridey. Her parents separated when she was four, and she was taken to Chicago to stay with an uncle and aunt. Living across the street was an Irish woman named Mrs Anthony Corkell, whose name before marriage was Bridie (spelt with an *ie*) Murphy.

Virginia's own mother's name was Katherine; Bridey's mother was Kathleen. One of the Corkell boys was called John, on whom the young Virginia had had a 'mad crush'; Bridey's husband was Sean, Gaelic for John. Bryan is the middle name of Virginia's husband; one of the given names of Bridey's husband was also Brian. Another Corkell boy was named Kevin, the same name as one of Bridey's friends. Virginia's own sister and Bridey both suffered a fall down the stairs.

Virginia had an Irish aunt who could speak with a good imitation of an Irish brogue and who used to regale her with stories about Ireland. There was also another woman who reputedly taught Virginia stage-Irish monologues. Virginia's uncle recalled how as a child Virginia used to dance jigs on the street for pennies; while under hypnotic trance Virginia once danced an Irish jig. Virginia had a brother who died when she was five; Bridey's brother died when Bridey was four.

A friend of Virginia's foster parents was a man whom Virginia affectionately called 'Uncle Plazz'; Bridey had an 'Uncle Plazz'. One of Virginia's favourite songs was *Londonderry Air* (Danny Boy); it was also Bridey's. Virginia admired red hair and had once dyed her own brown hair red; Bridey had flaming red hair. Virginia liked potato pancakes; so did Bridey. Several other minor parallels were also traced.

Virginia denied the truth of many of these so-called revelations, and in fact some of the findings could not be substantiated. To the present day, those who feel disposed to accept the Bridey Murphy story at its face value dispute the countervailing evidence. Those who reject the story feel that the truth about Bridey Murphy has been suitably exposed. No allegation of fraud was made about any of those involved. The fault, it was said, lay in attributing to a past incarnation what could satisfactorily be explained in terms of forgotten episodes in the present life of Virginia, which she had unconsciously reproduced under hypnosis, a commonplace occurrence known to any psychologist.

Whatever the merits and drawbacks of the book, it was in its own way a small landmark in social history. Thousands, indeed millions, of men and women of the western world who had never heard of reincarnation, or having heard dismissed it as so much nonsense, now began to give the subject some interested thought. It made people reincarnation-conscious.

Within two weeks the book had become a bestseller, and bookshops could barely keep up with demand. In less than six months it went through ten printings, amounting to more than 200,000 copies, to reach in time a total of over one million.

The book was serialized in over fifty newspapers, some of the papers reprinting the series twice over because of popular demand. It was translated into French, German, Italian, Dutch, Danish, Swedish, Spanish, Finnish and other languages, and in all was printed in more than thirty countries. It was made into a documentary movie by Paramount Pictures. A long-playing record made from a tape recording of one of Virginia's trance sessions, sold tens of thousands of copies.

Hostesses gave 'Come-as-You-Were' costume parties. Public bars sold Reincarnation Cocktails. There were records about reincarnation, songs and ballads about Bridey Murphy, even a Bridey Murphy Rock 'n' Roll. Books on hypnotism and reincarnation became the biggest craze in America. The services of nightclub hypnotists, who had long had difficulty in finding work, were now constantly sought.

People were being regressed back to ancient Egypt, Babylonia, China, even Atlantis and Arcadia. They lived again as prehistoric cave-men, and missing links. One lady described her existence in the year 1800 as a horse (Gardner, 1957, p.315). In Shawnee, Oklahoma, a teenage boy shot himself, leaving a note saying he could not wait to find out for himself the truth about Bridey Murphy, and now intended to investigate the facts in person.

Professor C.J. Ducasse, in evaluating the evidence for reincarnation in the Bridey Murphy case, concluded that it does not prove that Virginia is a reincarnation of Bridey, nor does it establish a particularly strong case for it. But it does suggest that in hypnotic trance paranormal knowledge seems to become manifest.

Dr Joseph B. Rhine, while admitting that there was nothing in the book that the student of science need take seriously, said that it has done some good in stimulating public curiosity about matters on the fringes of orthodox psychology, and thus paved the way for the more careful study of such phenomena.

**Arthur Guirdham**

Perhaps the most prolific contemporary advocate of reincarnation is Dr Arthur Guirdham (born 1905), English physician and psychologist, retired chief consultant in psychiatry of the Bath medical area, medical correspondent for the *Yorkshire Post*, and author of a series of books describing his existence in former times, especially thirteenth century France during the time of the Cathars.

Dr Guirdham first became interested in the subject of Catharism in 1938 when he read Ford Madox Ford's *Provence*, which, he says, 'acted as an enzyme', beginning a process of inner fermentation that continued for thirty years. He states that he had a 'burning desire' to go to Provence, and was 'haunted' by the longing to see Montségur, which was the scene of a terrible massacre of Cathars in 1244. During the Second World War he bought a large and detailed guide to Carcassonne, one of the great centres of Catharism.

Guirdham also became interested in Buddhism, a religion that accepts reincarnation as a basic tenet. He met, or was put in touch by friends who knew of his interests, with Tibetan lamas, theosophists, and people who shared his curiosity about the Cathars, Albigensians, the events at Montségur, the troubadours, Languedoc literature and Provençal history, and was given books on these subjects by his friends.

The best known of his own books, *The Cathars and Reincarnation*, was followed by book after book on the subject. *We Are One Another* describes how a group of people who lived and suffered together in thirteenth-century Languedoc, meet again in the twentieth century in the west of England. *The Lake and the Castle* describes the lives of the same group in various historical periods from fourth century Roman Britain to the present day. In addition, he has written *The Gibbet and the Cross*, a story about the extermination of the Cathars by the Crusaders, which however has the character of a novel. Finally, he wrote a book called *The Great Heresy*, a serious study of Catharism.

In the light of this it becomes difficult to understand

Dr Guirdham's statement that 'nobody can accuse me of a persistent and demanding obsession with the subject of Catharism' (Guirdham, 1970, p.53).

*The Cathars and Reincarnation* largely recounts the remarkable information given to Dr Guirdham from March 1962 by a patient, a young woman whom he calls Mrs Smith. Memories of their past life together came to her partly in dreams, and partly just drifted into her mind in random scraps, and they seemed to centre around Toulouse in thirteenth century France.

During a snowfall one day in January 1964, Dr Guirdham visited Mrs Smith to leave a message about a hospital appointment. Later, she told him that she had known he was coming, because the falling snow recalled the day when they had first met in the thirteenth century. She said that in that life he had been a man named Roger de Grisolles, and had one day come to their hovel near Toulouse and asked for shelter during a heavy snowstorm, and she had fallen instantly in love with him. As he lay asleep that night she crept over and kissed his hand.

Later they arranged meetings, but could not marry because he was of noble lineage and a Cathar, while she came of poor parents and was a Roman Catholic. Roger used to call her Puerilia. Although not married they started living together. She was eventually excommunicated by the church.

So far as the present writer is aware, the pseudonymous Mrs Smith has not been forthcoming for identification and questioning, as was Mrs Virginia Tighe the contemporary counterpart of Bridey Murphy. The information we have about her is thus necessarily limited. Dr Guirdham describes Mrs Smith at the time of their first meeting as in her early thirties, good-looking, open, communicative and smiling.

Mrs Smith was a busy housewife with a part-time job, but seems to have had a consuming love for writing. Her more mature graphophilic tendencies were a continuation of an early compulsion in this direction. As a schoolgirl she had had intimations of Catharism, and crammed her rough notebooks with her strange effusions. She started writing a novel, set in France, recording her life with Roger, pieced together from the fragments that streamed in on her or were revealed to her in dreams. A number of medieval French poems 'came over' to her in the same mysterious way.

Mrs Smith carried on what appears to have been a voluminous correspondence with Dr Guirdham, deluging him with her epistles, sometimes writing to him twice a week. At times she showed such precise knowledge relating to life in thirteenth century France and of the Cathars, that it astonished Dr Guirdham. Many of the little known particulars mentioned by her were subsequently confirmed by reputable authorities on medieval history.

Thus, she correctly drew the design of a medieval coin. She knew that medieval coins sometimes used to be cut in half. She stated that the colour of Cathar robes was not black, as the historians stated, but dark blue. She had a detailed knowledge of Cathar personalities. She was able to reproduce some of the favourite poems that Roger, who was the grandson of a troubadour, used to recite, which, Dr Guirdham surmises, came to her by 'clair-audience and far memory'.

Such details can be accounted for without much difficulty if presented in a different light. We are told elsewhere in the book that Mrs Smith collected and studied coins. The designs of coins, including those drawn by Mrs Smith, are to be found in illustrated books on numismatics. The fact that coins used to be cut in half may well have been known to her from similar sources. The difference between dark blue and black Cathar robes is not so considerable as to need emphasis, but in any event this information too can be gleaned from historical writings, how else could the authorities confirm that she was right? Runciman lists well over 100 modern works on Catharism and related subjects all published before 1940, and Guirdham too has his own extensive bibliography.

Detailed data on Cathar personalities and their families are available to any interested student. Guirdham himself states that 'very considerable' information on this line of research has been available for centuries. Mrs Smith read extensively on the Cathars, spent vacations in the Pyrenees from as early as 1957. She was in correspondence with world famous authorities on the subject of medieval history, consulted other specialists in the field, and had acquired an extraordinarily intimate knowledge of Catharism. She admits she had a photographic memory.

No information produced by her is so unusual as to warrant the belief that she was picking up the threads of knowledge she had acquired in an earlier incarnation, or tip the scales in favour of the hypothesis that her presumed 'clear vision' of past history was due to her former birth. 'Roger's songs' were in print and available for anyone to read, both in Provençal French and in English translation. That Mrs Smith read the songs as a schoolgirl and later forgot their source may strike some as perhaps a more likely explanation than that they floated into her consciousness word for word across the centuries.

Dr Guirdham, a sympathetic and magnanimous person, appears to feel more than disposed to take what she says at face value, without seeking alternative explanations. His book is liberally sprinkled with his generous acceptance of her statements: 'Mrs Smith was right'. 'Mrs Smith is once again dead accurate'. 'Mrs Smith is right as usual'.

Time and again Mrs Smith writes to Dr Guirdham that she has read the same book, or the same article on the same subject, or has had the identical thought on a certain subject as the doctor. It would seem that she had developed a feeling of warmth and attachment for the doctor, and she may have wished to demonstrate this for his benefit by suggesting similarities in their lives and experiences past and present. Dr Guirdham's interests and background were well enough known in the community in which he lived, and must have been known to Mrs Smith as well.

That she should recognize the doctor as her lover in a previous incarnation is to be noted. Colin Wilson writes, 'Surely this is one of those familiar cases of a patient falling in love with a doctor, and inventing a case history to make herself interesting?' (Smyth, 1970, Art.91). Although he rejects this hypothesis, it does seem that we have evidence here of the process known to psychologists as 'transference', in which one party in this form of dual relationship develops a strong feeling, usually of affection, towards the other.

It is relevant also to note how much of Mrs Smith's own background and interests correspond with the doctor's.

Both are of French ancestry. Both have names of French origin, and are familiar with the French language. He is drawn to and preoccupied with a place called Ashridge, in Hertfordshire, near the site of a thirteenth century monastery and a supposed Cathar enclave in England. Ashridge is the birthplace of her grandmother.

The doctor has Menière's syndrome, an affection of the inner ear described as a kind of epilepsy of the nerve of hearing which causes giddiness; sensitives are prone to be afflicted with it. She suffers from migraine, has spells of unconsciousness, and is considered an epileptic. He has periods of psychic activity and is deeply interested in ESP. She showed a faculty for ESP from the age of six, and has had several experiences of déjà vu.

Both have a sense of temporal dislocation and of 'being out of time'. Both are interested in the Cathars and in reincarnation. On several occasions Guirdham dates letters and notes 1264 instead of 1964. Both have intimations of a Cathar past, and write about it. In Mrs Smith's account Roger has a sad death from tuberculosis while in prison: Puerilia has a terrifying end at the stake.

The first time Mrs Smith sees the doctor she feels she recognizes him across the centuries. She writes to him of her early dreams, 'somehow, somewhere, you are involved'. The romantic note is introduced by the meeting in the snowstorm. Both have repeated nightmares about a tall man of menacing aspect. Both wake up screaming. The nightmares in both cases cease after Dr Guirdham and Mrs Smith meet.

The coincidence is surprising enough for Guirdham to comment on this last incident, 'The reader is entitled to his own interpretation'.

If one reader may venture an interpretation: could it be that some at least of these similarities were produced by Mrs Smith in an unconscious attempt, by means of an imaginary common background and shared memories, to provide evidence of a bond of spiritual kinship between them?

Some people may find a mediumship interpretation more acceptable. We have the case of Mrs Pearl Curran, to be given later, who produced factual historical material in her novels, without claiming them as reminiscences of her own past. Dr Guirdham himself points out that Mrs Smith took down the songs of Roger, 'rather as a spiritualist medium might operate'.

Certain passages in Guirdham's other books also indicate that information about his previous incarnations, so called, and those of other members of the group with whom his life was linked, was revealed to him by discarnate entities. In *The Lake and the Castle* spiritual 'presences' made themselves felt, and voices from the past were heard. The history of his Roman incarnation, for example, was obtained sometimes by 'direct contact with the revenants' and sometimes through a 'go-between' who served like a spiritualist medium, so that he was enabled to talk with the dead.

To the non-spiritualist the idea of telepathy might be more acceptable. There was clearly a genuine psychic rapport between Dr Guirdham and Mrs Smith, which was strengthened by her emotional attachment to him. The phenomenon of mind-picking is now an established fact of parapsychology. Dr Guirdham was deeply versed in Catharism and some of what he knew or felt may have been absorbed by her telepathically. The rest could have been acquired by diligent study, correspondence and hard work.

**Joan Grant**

Another writer who has produced voluminous evidence, if we can accept it as such, of previous incarnations, is Joan Grant (born 1907) who as a young woman could psychometrize, that is, pick up the psychic impressions surrounding objects, people and places. In her autobiographical *Time Out of Mind* she relates her own paranormal experiences.

She apparently has the faculty of being able to 'shift levels' of consciousness almost at will, and to recall phases of her earlier life-history in vivid detail. Once, on a visit to Egypt, she found herself strangely drawn to the ancient monuments, whose ruins saddened her as if for a departed glory she herself had known at first hand. Then a friend gave her a stone scarab (Egyptian beetle) and as soon as she touched it visions flooded into her mind of what she was convinced were episodes of her own past life. The material, thus received over a period of time, was embodied in her *Winged Pharaoh* (1937), the first of more than half a dozen historical novels which she claimed were 'biographies of previous lives'.

Joan Grant's memories go back to a very dim past. She states, 'I think I can remember an animal existence. But my earliest clear memories are of life 40,000 years ago in the age of the cave paintings' (Ebon, 1970, p.127). She also remembers her life as Sekeeta, daughter of a pharaoh of the first dynasty (*c.* 3300 B.C.), who herself later became pharaoh. This was the theme of her *Winged Pharaoh* mentioned above. In another book, *So Moses*

*Was Born*, she was again an Egyptian living in the Nile Valley. In *Return to Elysium* she describes her life in ancient Greece. She was also a minstrel lute player in sixteenth century Italy, described in *Life as Carola*. Her existence as an American Indian forms the subject of *The Scarlet Feather*. In a more recent incarnation she lived as an English girl named Lavinia, whose legs had been paralysed in a riding accident and who died in 1875.

In all Joan Grant recalls more than thirty previous incarnations, and tells of some of the ways in which she met her end in the past. She committed suicide because of unrequited love. She died of a mosquito bite. (She has, incidentally, written a scholarly work on mosquitoes.) She was burned at the stake as a witch – 'The wood was wet. It took an inordinately long time for the fire to kill me'. She was guillotined.

In 1958 Joan Grant met Denys Kelsey, the man who was to become her third husband. He was a doctor of medicine and a trained psychiatrist, and each instantly recognized the other, for they had shared lives before. During their Egyptian days, when he was an Egyptian captain, 'he was bitten on the eyelid by a fly, his face was terribly swollen'. In their Roman incarnation she committed suicide, because he, a young physician, did not return her love. Kelsey recalls his past as a charioteer in a chariot race in ancient Rome. They also lived before as husband and wife in eighteenth-century England.

Together Joan Grant and Denys Kelsey have evolved an age-regression therapy, where patients are led under hypnosis to project their minds back into their former lives and re-live the traumas of the past.

In the course of his practice Kelsey found that there were certain persistent neuroses that did not respond to orthodox methods. It seemed that childhood or infancy trauma, or psychological shock, was not always sufficient to account for the present mental condition of the patient. Joan Grant, who is able to 'pick up a resonance' and dramatically identify with a person, suggested that such neurotic conditions might be more deep-rooted, with a history going back beyond the current lifetime to an earlier critical experience.

In this far-memory therapy, described in their book *Many Lifetimes*, the patient is put under hypnosis and made to recall his earlier incarnations. A chosen key-word is sometimes used to start the process and the regression proceeds along the guidelines provided. The patient re-lives his past in a very vivid manner, speaking of it in the present tense and behaving as if he were actually undergoing the original experience.

This theory, they believe, may shed an entirely new light on some deep-seated human prejudices and fears, and sudden unaccountable animosities and attractions. According to Joan Grant many personal phobias such as the fear of falling, or drowning, or of sharp instruments, relate to a past life. Because of some traumatic event, usually terrifying in nature, certain fragments of the memory are trapped within the mind and a kind of festering process commences. If the condition is not healed these fragments are stored in the continuing memory, and may remain a permanent feature of the self. A warning signal is sent to the current conscious mind to be wary of any object or circumstance that was fatal to the self in the past.

Mostly, the impressions that continue to 'resonate' or re-echo in subsequent lifetimes are formed around certain basic emotional crises: those associated with an all-consuming love, fanatic hatred, feelings of tormenting jealousy or vengeance, or death by torture or violence. For example, in one case a man's aversion to touching feathers was traced back to a frightful experience in an earlier life, when vultures attacked and started tearing at him as he lay stricken and wounded on a battlefield.

**Dr Ian Stevenson**

A great deal of research into reincarnation has been undertaken by Dr Ian Stevenson, M.D., American psychologist born in Montreal in 1918, who is a professor of psychiatry and director of the department of parapsychology at the University of Virginia, Charlottesville.

In 1960, his 44-page essay, 'The Evidence for Survival from Claimed Memories of Former Incarnations', won the prize of the American Society for Psychical Research, given in honour of William James (d. 1910), one of its early presidents.

Stevenson had also initiated an international census of cases suggestive of reincarnation, and by 1973 twelve hundred examples had been collected from various parts of the world, and he and his colleagues recorded, examined, verified and analysed at first hand the evidence in several hundred of them.

During the 1960s, Stevenson personally investigated twenty such instances of alleged reincarnation: seven in India, three in Sri Lanka, two in Brazil, seven in Alaska, and one in the Lebanon. He paid numerous visits to these countries and interviewed scores of witnesses, pursuing each case with the pertinacity of a detective and examining the evidence in great detail with scientific impartiality. Several of these cases were followed up by him from time to time.

His published work on these investigations is a landmark in the history of the subject. The work is sober and scholarly, his doubts and queries are presented clearly and with fairness, and he is cautious in his analysis of the facts. He tabulates the evidence giving his own comments, and expresses his conclusions objectively. In the final analysis it would appear that the theory of reincarnation, as well as alternative theories, all have their shortcomings. Stevenson himself does not claim to have proved reincarnation, nor at this stage does he feel that he could opt for any one theory that could satisfactorily explain all the cases considered by him.

One case investigated by Stevenson at first hand might be summarized as an illustration.

In September 1949, a certain Ibrahim Bouhamzy died of tuberculosis in the Lebanese village of Khriby. Nine years later, in December 1958, in the village of Kornayel, about twenty-five miles away, and connected to Khriby by a winding mountain road, Imad Elawar was born. From the age of two Imad began referring to his earlier life in Khriby, to the various localities near by and to his friends and companions there.

He would describe this other life in meticulous detail, not in the imaginative way as would happen if the boy were making things up. He knew intimately the members of his 'other family', their habits and peculiarities, their favourite food and drink, their personal idiosyncrasies. It was also noticed that there were remarkable correspondences between the behavioural features of Imad and the character traits of the deceased Ibrahim.

Imad spoke feelingly of his beloved mistress, whom Stevenson refers to by the pseudonym Jamileh. He had loved her but was not allowed to marry her as she belonged to a lower class. The affair had caused considerable scandal in the community.

Jamileh had since married someone else and moved to another village.

Dr Stevenson was able to observe the case while it was still occurring in 1964, when Imad was just over five years old. He interviewed twenty relatives and friends associated with the two families involved, and paid several visits to the two villages. He travelled with Imad and his family to Ibrahim's village, and listed fifty-seven items recollected by the child. Ten out of these were recalled by the boy as they were being driven by car to Khriby; of these ten, three turned out to be incorrect; but of the remaining forty-seven items, he was wrong in only three instances. Altogether he was correct in fifty-one out of fifty-seven items, and the mistakes may have been due to his confusing memories of his present and past lives. In sixteen tests of recognition Imad failed one, and was somewhat vague in one, but was quite correct in fourteen.

**Joanne MacIver**

Besides his personal investigations, Dr Stevenson has also scrutinized and evaluated the evidence in many other reincarnation claims. One such case is that of Joanne MacIver, who in a previous life had apparently been Susan Ganier, an entity who died in 1903. Jess Stearn, a New York Journalist, investigated her case in collaboration with some other people and wrote a book about it.

Hypnotized by her father Ken MacIver, Joanne was regressed to recall her life as Susan Ganier in the middle of the last century on a Canadian farmstead, as well as other former lives. She was said to have mentioned names and localities which have since disappeared from most maps, though a few do survive in old deeds and records, and some were remembered by old settlers.

Yet the case as it stands is hardly sufficient to lend positive support to the theory of reincarnation. It would seem from the available evidence that Ken MacIver was consumed with the desire to prove reincarnation, and his daughter Joanne may have become subject to his suggestions. Stearn again could hardly have been an impartial witness, as we shall see when we look at the facts in a little more detail.

Ken MacIver, a Canadian government auditor, lived with his family in Orillia, a small town some eighty miles north of

Toronto. An experience at the age of five, when he was told that he would have to be born again before he could enter the kingdom of heaven, was, according to MacIver, his indoctrination into the whole concept of reincarnation. Already as a boy he had a keen sense of déjàism, and later in his youth had written some lines of verse about a past life.

He took up hypnosis at an early age, and was apparently familiar with at least some of the literature on reincarnation. Emboldened by his success in hypnotizing his daughter, MacIver began taking other subjects back to previous lives, including some to Atlantis. According to Stearn he soon became obsessed with reincarnation and lived for little else. He was fired with the idea of proving the truth of reincarnation right there in Orillia. He advertised in the Toronto *Star* asking for assistance in research of a case 'surpassing Bridey Murphy in importance' (Stearn, 1968, p.67).

Ever since his daughter's first regression he began pouring over provincial archives, and had sheaves of documents, letters and transcripts that he had collected for several years to corroborate his daughter's recollections. Not only was he constantly on the go, he took Joanne with him, scouring the countryside, tracking down old graves. It is possible that by the time other investigators came into the picture, Joanne was already well acquainted with names, places and history.

Joanne MacIver was born in 1948. She had always been psychic, felt she was unlike other children, and 'just knew' things she hadn't learnt, and even as a child had a strange sense of being grown up. She knew about reincarnation, and the subject of age regression was a current topic of conversation among the young people in her circle.

On 5 October 1962, Joanne and two friends were discussing hypnosis. Joanne tried to hypnotize a young man, failed to do so, and asked her father to try. He also failed with the boy but he noticed that during the attempt Joanne's eyes had closed in hypnotic sleep. She was successfully regressed, and after that there were numerous sessions, many of them being recorded on tape.

Little by little the story of her past life was pieced together. As Susan Ganier, she was born around 1835 in St Vincent Township, in Grey County, some ninety miles from Orillia. Susan had married a neighbouring farmer, Thomas Marrow, and settled near Sydenham Township. She survived her husband and died at the turn of the century.

Joanne also recalled her other lives. As Michael she had lived in a castle in France, date unspecified. Asked how he had died Michael replied, 'My mother had my head cut off'. Her earliest regression was to the year A.D. 748 when she was a Negro woman named O-I, who had lived in Africa and whose six children were eaten by ants.

It is more than likely that Jess Stearn, the New York journalist who took part in the search for confirmation of the story of the past lives of Joanne, came to the task already somewhat predisposed to believe in reincarnation. He had written a best-selling book on Cayce. He had met and talked with Virginia Tighe of Bridey Murphy fame. He had been interested in hypnotic age regression, and had watched the famous researcher, the late K.N. Jayatilleke of Sri Lanka, regress a subject under hypnosis.

He was 'convinced of the psychic', and the so-called sixth sense, and himself possessed a degree of ESP. On his arrival at Orillia he experienced a sense of déjàism, and had a distinct feeling that he had been there before. When he visited the neighbouring areas and the nearby lake, the sense of familiarity grew stronger.

But above all it was Joanne herself who captivated him. Describing his first impression of her he writes that she had a look that was 'ageless, endless, bottomless'. When he sat next to her he was again sharply aware of a sense of familiarity. He felt a bond with Joanne, and neither he nor she seemed to belong in that roomful of people. He was convinced that her innermost thoughts paralleled his own. For her part, when he asked her whether she had ever met anyone in the room before, she replied with a blush, 'Why, you— you knew that, of course' (Stearn, 1968, p.30).

Stearn was entranced by her 'bottomless blue eyes', and full of admiration for her beauty, her intelligence, the 'astonishing range of her mind', her 'inexplicable maturity', and although at times she seemed an unsophisticated adolescent, at other times she was a 'paragon of wisdom'.

Among the Orillians too there appears to have been a certain lack of healthy scepticism. The exception was perhaps

Dr Torrance, a physician, father of a school friend of Joanne's, who dubbed MacIver's claims as 'pure poppycock'.

One of the old settlers in the area who gave evidence was an octogenarian, Arthur Eagles, who stated that he had known Susan Ganier. But the deposition made by him to this effect could have been influenced by suggestions from MacIver. In any event Eagles had died some months earlier, at the age of eighty-six, before he could be interviewed by a more experienced team of researchers. A psychiatrist investigator regarded Eagles as a 'questionable source'.

Checking the data that came up in Joanne's regressions proved wellnigh impossible. No provincial death records existed prior to 1879. There was in fact considerable difficulty in checking anything before the turn of the century. The search for corroborative evidence and landmarks was therefore 'frustratingly unrewarding' (Stearn, 1968, p.35).

Some of the data checked roughly, but much of it was inconsequential, contradictory, and consisted of trivia. A few of the surnames mentioned by Joanne were common enough in the district, but others were quite unknown and could not be identified or traced.

Here again, it is possible that some of the names could have been telepathically picked up by Joanne from her father, or from other local residents. As Stearn himself points out, names have been picked out at random from the past through clairvoyance.

Dr Stevenson who flew up to Canada to study the case, found it 'tantalizing and intriguing', but too fragmentary to prove reincarnation. It was exceedingly difficult to rule out ESP or even normal channels by means of which Joanne might have picked up some of her 'memories' (Ebon, 1970, p.119).

**Edward W. Ryall**

Another case that has interested Dr Stevenson is that of Edward W. Ryall, author of *Second Time Round*, to which Stevenson has written an introduction and an appendix containing notes on the verification of details in the book.

Ryall was born in England in 1902, and remembers his life as John Fletcher, a yeoman farmer in the west country, and his premature and violent death in a skirmish just before the battle of Sedgemoor in Somersetshire, where the forces of James II defeated the Duke of Monmouth in 1685.

Ryall's book contains a wealth of detail not known to any but students of the period, including many allusions to objects (agricultural, commercial and domestic), to local customs and events, along with words and idiomatic expressions current at the time. He also made an accurate sketch of the route taken by the Duke of Monmouth's army on the night march to the scene of the forthcoming battle.

From early childhood Ryall had intimations of his previous incarnation, and often came up with dialect words unknown to the family. In 1910, when he was eight years old he had a clash with his father. Ryall senior had taken the lad out into the garden to show him the spectacle of Halley's comet then visible in the night sky, whereupon the child said that he had seen it before a long time ago, much to the annoyance of his father. One of the boy's memories had in fact been that of showing the comet to *his* son in 1682.

Sometimes Ryall seemed to be transported for shorter or longer intervals without any effort on his part, and would find himself in the surroundings and among the people of his earlier life. On occasion, while he could watch them and understand what they were saying to one another, he himself was not visible. No one seemed to notice his presence, and this rather upset him.

The facts that are to be set against the theory of recall and reincarnation in this case are the following.

English history is so well documented that possibly all the details mentioned by Ryall were already published in specialized books and papers. Maps and plans of the battle, as well as historical novels of the time relating to the incidents he describes, were also available. This does not imply fraud on Ryall's part, as Stevenson himself rightly makes clear. But the fact of cryptomnesia and mind-tapping, which we shall examine later, could well account for some of the narrative details.

Stevenson admits that Ryall had a 'quite superior memory'. In his student days Ryall 'read extensively', including a textbook summary of the Monmouth rebellion and the battle of Sedgemoor. Ryall was a non-commissioned officer in the Second World War. In the course of their correspondence Stevenson discovered that Ryall also showed 'a most creditable knowledge' of Hindu religious customs, and Provençal poetry. Before he began to write *Second Time Round* Ryall had also read Stevenson's *Twenty Cases*, and had twice visited the area of Somersetshire, the county where the battle had taken place.

Stevenson anticipates the reader's doubts when he says that Ryall writes so well that the reader might be tempted to say that the book 'reads like a novel', although he also makes it clear that he would not like Ryall's book to be classed with other historical novels supposedly based on memories of past lives. It should be mentioned that when Ryall was writing his book he was not in a state of trance, either hypnotic or mediumistic, but wide awake.

While Stevenson presents the facts to be taken into account for a proper assessment of the narrative, and his own conclusion is in favour of reincarnation, he reserves the right to modify his opinions if further evidence shows that another interpretation is more feasible (Ryall, 1974, p.28).

### The Bloxham Tapes

What has been called the most extraordinary evidence for reincarnation is supposed to have been provided by the now famous Bloxham tapes, the regressions recorded by Mr Arnall Bloxham, a hypnotherapist of Cardiff, who believes that scores of his subjects under hypnosis remembered and re-lived their previous lives. A television producer, Jeffrey Iverson, has written a book about the experiments, and a documentary film has been made of the taped material.

During the past twenty years Bloxham tape-recorded over 400 examples of reincarnation. He has thousands of feet of recordings, much of the material dull and uninteresting, but some of it regarded by experts as providing conclusive proof of reincarnation.

Bloxham had a grammar-school education. He did naval service in both World Wars, holding the rank of naval lieutenant in the Second World War. Originally he had intended to become a doctor, and started training as a doctor in India, but a bout of typhoid cut short his medical career, and led him to concentrate on hypnotherapy.

At the same time he has been fascinated with the fringe areas, and deeply interested in eastern and occult philosophy, and the law of karma. From his childhood he was convinced of his own earlier incarnation, and says, 'I had always felt that I had lived before' (Smyth, 1970, Art. 33). He had an experience of déjàism and throughout his life held to his belief in rebirth, his faith being confirmed by his study of reincarnation in the east.

Dr Bloxham's experiments in regression began late in his career, for it was only in 1956 that he decided to use hypnosis to unlock memories of past lives. His first experiment was carried out on a young schoolteacher named Ann Ockenden, who readily entered into hypnotic trance and was eventually regressed to seven different lives. Bloxham's wife, Dulcie, in order to make his work better known, described the sittings in a book entitled, *Who Was Ann Ockenden?*

Another of Bloxham's more notable subjects was Jane Evans, born in 1939, who was able to recall six previous lives, the earliest as a woman who lived in England about A.D. 286 near Eboracum or Roman York. The most interesting of her regressions was as Rebecca, a Jewess of York, who came to a violent end in 1190 during a massacre of the Jews.

Jane Evans is a lively and intelligent woman, seemingly of Jewish stock herself, who attended high school, studied history, French and Latin, but not to an advanced level. She read about Greece and Tibet, and although she never mentioned these two countries, she was interested in ancient times and eastern religions.

Professor Barrie Dobson, Reader in History at the University of York, whose history of the Jewish massacre of 1190 in York had recently been published (did Jane read this book?) was of the opinion that although the language used by Rebecca belonged more to the twentieth century than to medieval England, the account was 'true to what we know of the events and times themselves' (Iverson, 1977, p.44).

Another notable subject of Bloxham's is Graham Huxtable, a man from Swansea, who regressed two centuries to his life as a gunner's mate on *HMS Aggie*, a frigate under Captain Pearce, then engaged in blockading the coast of Napoleonic France. He recalled dramatically a fight with a French ship off Calais, using archaic slang, and spoke of practices on board ship which are now obsolete. The mate's leg was shot away by cannon fire, and the subject re-lived the agony with harrowing intensity.

Huxtable gave so many unusual details about naval life at the time, that Earl Mountbatten (d. 1979) borrowed the tape to play back to experts on naval history. It should be noted that there is no record of any ship named *HMS Aggie*, and it is impossible to identify any Captain Pearce who skippered a British frigate in the circumstances described.

Bloxham's subjects have also included the usual sprinkling of crusaders, witches, monks, nuns, courtiers, mercenaries and Cromwellian soldiers. One throwback claimed that he had spoken with 'the Nazarene', that is, Christ. Another lived as Elizabeth I, and described, with no historical warrant, Sir Walter Raleigh making love to her in the cabin aboard Raleigh's ship.

Since the historic day when Morey Bernstein brought Bridey Murphy into existence, scores of enthusiastic researchers have attempted to unravel the genealogy of willing souls, and it might be thought that the human past is now open for inspection to any hypnotist with a tape recorder. But as more serious students begin to probe deeper into the mysteries of hypnotic age regression, they, like Stevenson, find it increasingly difficult to resist the conclusion that there might be more than one explanation for the curious data that emerge from subjects in trance.

In their book, *Lives to Remember*, Peter Underwood, psychical researcher, and Leonard Wilder, dentist and hypnotist, relate how an English housewife, Peggy Bailey, re-lived three different lives. These sessions too were recorded on tape. She was in turn Sally Fraser, who lived in eighteenth century Devon; Liza Bloggs, who lived in the nineteenth century; and finally, Lady Alice Browning, who lived in the early part of the present century.

Here again we find a knowledge of places known neither to the subject in the waking state, nor to the hypnotist; the use of colloquial words and phrases appropriate to the period in question; a distinct change of voice and accent; and a remarkable histrionic talent beyond the subject's conscious capability. In the book each regression is described by Wilder, and this is followed by a balanced 'Assessment and Discussion' by Underwood. In conclusion both authors rightly agree that a lot more evidence is desirable before reincarnation can be accepted as a proven fact (Underwood and Wilder, 1975, p.214).

In a still more impressive book, *Encounters with the Past*, subtitled, 'How Man can Experience and Relive History', written by a historian and broadcaster, Peter Moss, in collaboration with a hypnotherapist, Joe Keeton, the authors record the stories of seven of their more remarkable cases. Joe Keeton skilfully leads his subjects into the past with such suggestions as: 'Time is running backwards and you are free to choose a character in the immensity of all time'. The regressed subject provides facts of which he normally has no knowledge in his conscious state, including names of people and places, expressions and modes of speech current at the time, and little-known historical details.

Research into old parish registers and other relevant documents confirmed that some of the material received from the subjects was indeed correct. A number of statements were classed as fortunate guesses, and some were only partly right. Others were half-truths or near misses. There were also the usual anachronisms and inconsistencies. Some of the data was wrong and much of it trivial. The brief epilogue of the book, which seems to summarize the authors' conclusions, leaves the reader with a series of unanswered questions.

It would appear then, from the evidence as it stands today, that it is still too early to opt unreservedly for reincarnation, for this effectively closes the door to several alternative, and, in the view of some researchers, perhaps more feasible, options. In a later chapter we shall consider a few of these alternatives.

# 4

# The Case For Reincarnation

We have seen that reincarnation is an ancient and widespread belief, and a number of reasons have been advanced in support of it.

In the view of modern exponents it is entirely in consonance with the idea of evolution, and of human progress and perfectibility. According to the theory of biological evolution, man's body has evolved over millions of years, making a long and gradual ascent from the lower species. Such a theory must run hand in hand with that of man's mental evolution, and, if we believe in a transcendental reality beyond ours, of his spiritual evolution as well. The soui like the body must be given time to evolve, and reincarnation would seem to provide the time and opportunity for man's spiritual self-perfection.

The soul is too vast an entity to complete its education and purify itself after one short span on earth. It must have a varied schooling in many lives, returning each time to fresh endeavour. Perfection is a long process, requiring more than one lifetime to achieve, since one brief sojourn here clearly cannot afford sufficient opportunity for the individual's full maturity, or be adequate preparation for an eternal life hereafter.

Although we are, in a sense, animals in our infancy, we come prepared by our own past, having acquired from our previous lives much that is utterly beyond the scope of animals. We grow up capable of speech, of understanding, of humour, of love, with a certain 'appetite' for higher things, in touch with our past and conscious of our future, and this represents the potential for further growth.

The case for reincarnation has been set forth on various

grounds. It has been claimed, above all, as a thoroughly rational and sensible doctrine. W.R. Inge (d. 1954), Dean of St Paul's, London, perhaps expressed the view of many people when he said, 'I find the doctrine both credible and attractive' (Johnson, 1953, p.382).

According to the principle of conservation, nothing in the universe can go to waste. There is often a deep personal conviction in this matter, such as a man might have at the end of a hard and useful life, that the wisdom and experience he has gained, can surely not be dissipated with his death.

Furthermore, reincarnation seems to explain in a logically acceptable manner the many otherwise inexplicable situations that exist in the world. It solves the riddle of our present lot, and provides a satisfactory reason for some unanswered questions about the inequities of life: the prosperity of the wicked, the misery of the virtuous, the unfulfilled lives of those who die young, the tragic destiny of innocent children born with some serious physical handicap. It explains the mysteries of sin and suffering, and the apparent injustice in lives 'widely and cruelly differentiated'.

The unscrupulous business magnate who brings unhappiness and distress to others by his sharp practices, and lives in peace and comfort to the end of his days, is a common example of the disturbing injustice we see around us. Does he get away with it? The poor woman who works hard to bring up her children, yet dies forsaken and neglected by them, is another. Does her life of love and sacrifice go unrewarded? Does the callous indifference of her children go unpunished?

John Dryden (d. 1711) wrote, 'Virtue in distress and vice in triumph make atheists of mankind'. The theory of reincarnation, completely exonerates God from the charge of injustice, favouritism, malice, cruelty or caprice.

It is sometimes stated by non-reincarnationists that the wicked will receive their retribution and the virtuous their reward in the spiritual realms hereafter, and will make all further progress in those realms. But then, it might be asked, what was the purpose of being born in this world at all? Does not our earth-life become meaningless? Why cannot we all have our probation and testing carried out in a gradual series of wholly spiritual existences?

The reincarnationist argues that nothing is so fitted for the retributive process as life on the material plane, where the defects or virtues of the individual are manifested. In one case, it is said, a woman who was deceived and ill-treated by her husband whom she loved and trusted, discovered under regression that in an earlier life, she had deceived and been unfaithful to a loving and trusting husband. In another instance a man who was betrayed had himself betrayed people in the past. A cripple in this life was found to have been responsible for crippling someone in a past life.

Digestive ailments have been traced to gluttony before. One blind musician learned from an adept that in an earlier life as a despot in the ancient middle east he used to blind his enemies with red-hot irons. A woman who suffered from persistent migraine was told by a psychic whom she consulted that in a previous incarnation she had lived as a man during the French Revolution and had been responsible for the beheading of several innocent victims.

It is believed that karmic repercussion may also assume a symbolic guise. For example, a woman who in an earlier life had been extremely haughty towards others was reborn as a man of extremely short stature so that others, quite literally, 'looked down' on him. In a hypothetical example given by Gina Cerminara, a person who had caused witches to be ducked in water, might perhaps suffer from enuresis (bed-wetting) in another incarnation.

A number of deep psychological problems that are inexplicable, in terms of traditional diagnostic concepts can, it is believed, be resolved by a better understanding of the laws governing reincarnation. Thus one's sex or one's attitude to sex in the preceding life, often determine one's gender in the present life. A person who was unhappy with his sex in one life might have another sex in this life. Transsexualism, in which a person feels that he is of the sex opposite to that of his outward sexual appearance, and transvestism, the uncontrollable desire to wear clothes appropriate to the sex opposite to one's own, have been explained as the continuing memory of a different and happy sexual experience in a previous life. Men with pronounced feminine characteristics and women with distinct male characteristics, as well as homosexuals in all ranges may be motivated by powerful subconscious impulses flowing in from their earlier life experiences, when they were of the opposite sex.

Reincarnation has been called 'the master key to the problem of heredity'. It has been invoked to explain the curious inheritance of habits, personality traits, postures, gestures. Physical weakness in some organ or part of the body, deformity, a tendency to certain sicknesses, even personal preferences and aversions, are taken as indicating a carry-over from one's past. Dr Jamuna Prasad, Deputy Director of Education in Uttar Pradesh, India's largest state, reported the case of the man who recalled that in an earlier life he had been over-fond of milk curd, and how one day he had choked to death while swallowing a mouthful. In the present life his dislike of milk curd was so intense that he would get ill at the mere sight of it.

In the reincarnationist view everything in our present life is meaningful, and one should therefore accept every adversity, setback or failure as a guiding light. Any persistently-held attitude of intolerance, distrust or anxiety might have its origins in a past life. Any deep complexes, compelling intuitions, unaccountable feelings, recurrent dreams, irrational fears and hatreds, persistent phobias and mental obsessions should be explored in this light to discover their source. They may point to a karmic complex with roots in a previous life, and if not properly understood could hold back the eventual development of the spirit.

Some psychologists have claimed that certain ailments cannot be explained entirely by physical drawback or organic defect in the present life of the sufferer. Joan Grant, for instance, finds that some incident in a past incarnation is frequently best able to account for the present pain or illness of the patient.

Dr Blanche Baker, Ph.D., M.D., of San Francisco, who feels that the theory of reincarnation is entirely credible, has experimented with a modified version of Freud's free-association method to revive past-life memories and so release patients from psychosomatic illness.

Dr Guirdham's book, *The Psyche in Medicine*, is almost wholly devoted to sponsoring the idea that a great many of the diseases from which we suffer are a direct result of some critical incident in our previous lives. In fact he categorically declares, 'There is no disease known to man the cause of which is entirely determined in what is called his own lifetime' (Guirdham, 1978, p.147).

The presence of birthmarks (naevi), moles, warts and weals on the body of a child, especially if they are like those borne by a deceased ancestor, and duplicate them in size and location, are sometimes regarded as tokens of rebirth. Particularly significant are scars or similar marks due to what would appear to be an accident or injury that could not have been sustained by the infant in his present life.

In certain parts of the world such birthmarks are often regarded as a sure sign that an earlier progenitor has been born again. In a famous case in India, personally investigated by the Mogul emperor Aurangzeb (d. 1707), the individual concerned had birthmarks exactly corresponding to those of an earlier entity, and this, added to the other features present in the case, confirmed, in the minds of many witnesses, that genuine reincarnation was involved.

The same peculiar significance of birth and other marks was also stressed among the native inhabitants of Alaska. Writing in the middle of the last century, the Russian bishop of Alaska, I.E.P. Veniaminov, said that the Tlingits always paid close attention to any birthmarks on the body of a newborn baby. If the child bore marks, scars or moles resembling those borne by a deceased relative, it was taken for granted that that person had returned to earth, and they gave the child the name of the deceased.

Dr Ian Stevenson who quotes these and similar instances has studied several such cases at first hand, and also records a number recently reported by other researchers. A Tlingit fisherman in Alaska named William George aged sixty years, expressed his intention of returning to earth, and repeatedly said to his son and daughter-in-law before he died that he would return as their son, and that two prominent pigmented moles, one on his left shoulder and one on the left forearm, would be duplicated in the next incarnation. Nine months after his disappearance at sea in 1949 during a fishing expedition, his daughter-in-law had a baby boy, with moles in the identical places (Stevenson, 1974, P.232).

Again, a boy born with a gash-scar on his right side said that in a previous life he had been killed by a spear. Relatives later confirmed that the boy's uncle had indeed been killed by such a weapon being thrust in his side (Greenhouse, 1973, p.207).

From England comes the strange case of the children of Mr and Mrs John Pollock, of Whitley Bay, Northumberland. In 1956 their two daughters, Joanna, eleven, and Jacqueline, six, were run over and killed by a car. Seventeen months later, in 1958, Mrs Pollock became pregnant, and Mr Pollock began to think in terms of the girls being reborn. In due course Mrs Pollock gave birth to twin girls, Gillian, the elder by four minutes, and the younger, Jennifer.

According to the Pollocks, the twins had some striking 'memory hangovers' with regard to their past lives. Besides, Jennifer had a white scar across her forehead exactly duplicating a scar the dead Jacqueline had had, the result of a fall when she was three years old; and Jennifer also carried a distinctive birthmark above her left hip, as had Jacqueline (Stearn, 1968, p.86).

Also put forward as an important factor in support of reincarnation is the curious phenomenon of déjàism (French, *déjà*, 'already'), the feeling that one has already seen, heard or experienced something before, although it is actually being experienced for the first time. It has the quality of recognition rather than simple recall.

Such phenomena are usually concerned with things seen, and are known by the blanket term, *déjà vu*, 'already seen', but they are by no means restricted to sight. Thus we have *déjà lû*, 'already read, *déjà entendu*, 'already heard', *déjà éprouvé*, 'already experienced, *déjà senti*, 'already felt', *déjà aimé*, 'already loved', all of which are forms of re-encounter, real or imagined, with the past.

Déjàism is not confined to mystics, but has been the experience of ordinary people in all walks of life: lawyers, businessmen, mechanics, nurses, soldiers, engineers, school teachers. Most people have had moments when some perfectly commonplace incident touches a chord which seems to set up distant reverberations as if from some dimly remembered past. There are occasional glimmerings of memory, faint traces of recollection that flash upon the mind's eye from the innermost recesses of the unconscious, recalling and recapturing a momentary vision of something known before. As Dante Gabriel Rossetti (d. 1882) wrote, 'Some veil did fall – I knew it all of yore'.

In *déjà vu* a person has a feeling, on finding himself in some place he consciously knows he has never previously seen, that he has in fact visited it already, and can often prove it by describing it down to the last detail. It may be a landscape, a stretch of road, or a house on a hill that suddenly strikes him as familiar. In some cases a curious sense of depersonalization and unreality accompanies the experience. The things around one become undefined and vague as if one were slipping into another dimension or plane of existence, and the strong feeling of the 'historicity' of the event now being witnessed strikes the mind. The sensation, brief but vivid, is that 'one has been here before'.

The Swiss psychologist Carl Gustav Jung (d. 1961) described déjàism as 'a historic excerpt from which the preceding and succeeding text is missing'. He himself actually believed that he had had a parallel life in the eighteenth century.

Typical of the more dramatic déjà vu experience is one cited by Sir Alexander Cannon, of a young bride on her honeymoon trip up the Danube. She had never been to that part of the world yet felt strongly that she was familiar with it all. She described the scenery and landscape before they got to it. At one point she insisted that she disembark, and was so fretful and uneasy that her husband was persuaded to pay heed. She led her husband to an old unoccupied castle, begged the caretaker to let them in, found her way unerringly through the rooms and corridors until she came to a locked door, and pointing to it as the room where she had been murdered, collapsed in a dead faint. That part of the castle had not been used for years, and when opened the chamber was found to contain two skeletons, with a rusty dagger on the floor (Cannon, 1970, p.37).

The inexplicable attraction that people sometimes have for a particular period of history, for a certain foreign country, for a certain lauguage, has also been attributed to déjàism, the pull of a forgotten memory out of a past incarnation. The German businessman and amateur archaeologist, Heinrich Schliemann (d. 1890) was irresistibly drawn to ancient Greece, and as if by instinct unerringly discovered the site of ancient Troy, where many experts had failed before him. Was it the pull of an age-old association?

Again, could the two remarkably different personalities, English and Arab, of T.E. Lawrence (d. 1935), perhaps be explained in terms of reincarnation? It is claimed that in some cases the bonds that link one to the past might be strong enough to affect even the appearance of a person. The French scholar Jean François Champollion (d. 1832) who completed the decipherment of the famous Rosetta Stone which helped in unravelling the mystery of ancient Egyptian hieroglyphics, had a sallow, almost brown complexion and remarkably oriental features and was curiously Egyptian in appearance.

It has been suggested that people who are unaccountably repelled by certain individuals or take an instant dislike to some perfectly harmless stranger, may also perhaps be stirred by the unconscious recollection of an unpleasant encounter with them in a previous life. Similarly they may feel powerfully drawn to others by the deep-rooted pull of earlier affinities.

Romantic literature is filled with stories on the theme of *déjà aimé*, 'already loved', where two people fall instantly and madly in love at first sight, and give up family, home, wealth, and even risk their lives, to be united with each other. It is as though they had loved centuries earlier and were only waiting for the moment to meet again, so that they could continue their great love, and so fulfil their destiny.

What can be made of such cases? Reincarnationists hold that they represent clear proof of rebirth. Sceptics remain unconvinced.

The whole concept of déjàism can be extended to cover an even wider area of human activity and behaviour. The French philosopher René Descartes (d. 1650) spoke of certain innate ideas or clear truths, which are present in the mind at birth. Like the instinct of animals, men seem to possess an anterior memory that reveals itself in their strange intuitions and predispositions, their inbuilt talents and insights, and their inspirations, suggestive of promptings from some earlier rehearsals. It is as though they were a remembrance of experiences 'not lost in death, as not in birth acquired', as the poet Arthur Hugh Clough (d. 1861) expressed it.

The understanding and wisdom of men is often deeper and embraces a wider range than could possibly be gleaned from the exertions of a single brief lifetime. The proficiency acquired after long struggle, the skills built up by strenuous effort, the faculties cultivated by their own exertions, and the qualities they have made their own by self-sacrifice and study, do not just vanish when they die. They awaken from the sleep of death in a new body, and at their birth the veil that fell across their vision is gradually lifted, and they see with the experience of the past.

Each embodiment is progressive. Nothing is lost. There is a continuous accumulation and preservation of skills and knowledge. Children especially are known to have a large fund of innate talent at their disposal that cannot entirely be accounted for by heredity, environment, cerebral activity, education, hormones or training. They would appear to be living evidence, in the words of the Cambridge Platonist, Henry More (d. 1687), 'that these souls did once subsist in some other state'. Knowledge is reminiscence. The lessons learnt in the school of a past life are brought to the classrooms of the present life. What we might regard as genius, or a lucky gift, or a natural, easy aptitude for things, may be the fruit of hard work in a previous incarnation.

The fact that children can often grasp complex facts speedily and without prolonged instruction, suggests that they may be recalling them rather than acquiring them for the first time. It is as though they recapitulate in a short time all the earlier stages of their progress. Not all learning is due to teaching. Exceptional talent is practical evidence of past aptitudes, as when a precocious child reveals a rare gift, or an infant prodigy manifests some extraordinary endowment. They are believed simply to be picking up at the point where they had left off in the earlier existence.

In ancient Greece the followers of Pythagoras also held that exceptional talent was rooted in a past life. In support they related the legend of the learned Greek chief Palamedes, who had accompanied the Greeks in their campaigns against Troy and who was said to have added certain letters to the then incomplete Greek alphabet. According to the story he was reborn in the time of Apollonius of Tyana (d. A.D. 98), a thousand years later, and from birth had a knowledge of writing.

Some children exhibit a quite unusual premature development of their mental faculties; they perform startling intellectual feats or display outstanding artistic gifts that defy explanation. The particular aptitudes that appear most often in such cases are for music, languages, chess and mathematics, especially calculation. Hundreds of such prodigies are named in historical annals and the list makes impressive reading, as the following brief selection will show.

Christian Heinecken (d. 1725) of Germany, was said to have talked within a few hours of being born. At the age of one he knew the principal events related in the Pentateuch; at two he knew the whole of Bible history; at three he had mastered the outlines of world history and geography, and spoke Latin and French in addition to his native German. In 1724 the King of Denmark, sceptical of what he had heard about the boy, sent for him, and was astounded to receive first-hand confirmation of his learning. The child predicted his own death, which took place one year later, at the age of four.

Jean Cardiac (d. 1726) French prodigy, started learning the alphabet when only three months old, and before he died at the age of seven was proficient in French, Latin, English, Greek, Hebrew, and had a good knowledge of arithmetic, history, geography and heraldry.

Philippe Baratier (d. 1740) when only four could speak German, French and Latin, translated the Greek Bible at the age of five, was a member of an ecclesiastical synod in Berlin at the age of six, of the Royal Academy of Berlin at eight, and a doctor of philosophy at the age of fourteen.

George Frederick Handel (d. 1759) played the clavichord when only an infant, was already famous at five, a composer in his own right at eight, and gave concerts at the age of nine.

Wolfgang Amadeus Mozart (d. 1791) seemed to have been born an accomplished musician. He composed minuets and wrote a sonata at four, and an opera at seven.

Gottfried Mind (d. 1815) from early boyhood was known throughout Europe for his delightful paintings of household pets and children. But few knew that he was actually a moron and had to be accompanied by a nurse at all times.

Ludwig van Beethoven (d. 1827) played in public at the age of eight, and had his compositions published at nine.

Franz Schubert (d. 1828) composed songs and quartets at the age of eleven.

Evariste Galois (d. 1832) French prodigy, one of the most outstanding geniuses in the history of mathematics, whose teenage papers, now recognized as being of unusual merit, were at the time rejected by the academics as incomprehensible. He was killed in a duel at the age of twenty-one. The night before, he had hurriedly jotted down a few of his mathematical discoveries, some of which were not understood and appreciated until fifteen years, and some only twenty-five years after his death.

Zerah Colborn (d. 1840) son of an American carpenter displayed astonishing arithmetical powers from the age of five. He could answer immediately questions to which no known rules applied, and discovered certain properties of numbers which were unknown till then.

Frederic Chopin (d. 1849) played at public concerts before he was nine and published his first work at fifteen.

Johann Dahse (d. 1861), or Dase, a German boy who could not get the first principles of mathematics into his head and was baffled by geometry, but whose brain made instant computer-like calculations. He could, for instance, mentally multiply two numbers of 100 digits each. On the recommendation of Karl Friedrich Gauss, the greatest mathematician of his day, he received a grant from the Academy of Sciences in Hamburg, so that his natural talent could be exploited. In the next twelve years he had worked out a series of tables of logarithms, factors and prime numbers that few mathematicians could have accomplished in a lifetime (Barlow, 1951, p.37).

Vito Mangiamele (d. 1865), illiterate Sicilian shepherd, was produced before the French Academy at the age of ten and astonished them with his instantaneous answers to difficult questions in mathematics.

George Bidder (d. 1878) was born in a village in Devonshire and later became a great civil engineer. When still a lad of five he could work out in few seconds complicated sums in multiplication and division, involving dozens of figures.

James Clerk Maxwell (d. 1879) Scottish mathematician and physicist, had his first mathematical paper read before the Royal Society at the age of fifteen. It was described as superior to Sir Isaac Newton's treatment of the same problem.

William Siddis (d. 1880), American, could read and write at the age of two; at eight was fluent in English, Russian, German, Latin and Greek; and at eleven lectured on the subject of the fourth dimension to a gathering of professors.

Paul Morphy (d. 1884), American, learned chess at ten, three years later beat the U.S. champion, and then proceeded to beat the current world champion.

Tom Wiggins (d. 1907) better known as Blind Tom, a Negro

slave of Alabama, had never touched a piano till he was four years old. One day he sat down at his master's piano, moving his fingers over the keys, and after a few errors found the right chords as if by instinct. It took him only a few minutes to get his bearings and he then went on to play the instrument like a professional.

José Capablanca (d. 1942), Cuban, was already a brilliant chess player at the age of four, seldom lost a game even when playing with experts who had taken years to perfect their moves, and went on to become world champion.

Jacques Inaudi (d. 1950), Italian boy of little education could do complicated sums in his head. He was once matched against three calculating machines which were set to work on three different problems, and he came up with the answers first.

One of the arguments put forward by those who oppose the theory of reincarnation, is that except for adepts and a few rare souls, people ordinarily do not remember either their past incarnations or their intercarnate existence, that is, the interval between death and rebirth. If we are to benefit from the errors of our past lives, we should in all fairness be allowed to recall them.

To this a number of answers have been given. To start with, there is the shattering experience of death in the previous incarnation which obliterates much of the memory of what has happened to us. Again, in the new life, the mind is prepared for fresh experiences, and the trauma of birth effectively erases much of what came before.

It is also to be remembered that the body, the seat of the sense organs, and the instrument of our involvement with the material world, may be as much a hindrance as a help in our ability to recall the past. Perhaps the remembrance of our earlier life would enormously complicate our present life. It would cause needless confusion to have to live with the problems of more than one life at a time.

The experiences of each life are part of the process of our education, and having reached a certain level it is not necessary that we should remember the stages by which we reached it. We do not remember the early stumbling efforts by which we learned to walk, talk, read or write. It has also been argued that recollection would hinder probation. The soul's struggle from life to life must be isolated from the distracting influences of its past.

Again, it is pointed out that forgetfulness of our previous life need not preclude the idea of one continuing entity. For example, we do not remember anything of our infancy, or of much of our childhood, or of considerable segments of our immediate past as adults. We spend about one third of our lives in sleep and remember almost nothing of it when we wake up. Yet we know that the infant and the adult, the sleeper and the waker are one and the same person. We cannot be expected to recall the remote yesteryears of our varied existences, and the fact of our forgetting what happened does not alter the fact of our continuing identity.

On the other hand there are those who maintain that we do remember our past. Although it may be beyond recall by conscious effort it is stored in our unconscious or deep memory. Amnesia is never complete. We do not suffer total oblivion, and never quite forget everything. A host of particular memories and more than a vestige of the past remain with us.

Some people believe that during the later stages of development within the womb, the foetus has a clear remembrance of its past history, but the memory of it begins progressively to diminish after birth. As William Wordsworth (d. 1850) wrote in his great Platonic ode, 'Our birth is but a sleep and a forgetting'. The occasional intimations that the child has of its earlier existence slowly recede and fade as he grows up, and may be totally obliterated from the conscious mind as he becomes increasingly preoccupied with material concerns and finds himself involved with the realities of practical life. In a way it may be said that we fail to remember because of our neglect, or the weakness, of our spiritual senses.

Some personal memories of former incarnations are said to be spontaneously recalled by all of us, although most fail to recognize them as such. Of the minority who claim to do so, a few have written accounts of their former lives in the form of novels, giving authentic details of historical times. There are besides the alleged cases of liberated souls who are credited with the ability to recall previous incarnations, their own as well as those of others, by specially developed yogic powers or occult techniques.

Furthermore, there is the curious phenomenon of xenoglossis, where a person, usually in trance, suddenly starts using archaic words, or speaking in an unknown tongue, or in a foreign language he has never learnt, or perhaps never even heard of. This is sometimes brought out as convincing evidence of the recall of information from a former life.

Thus, a young Swiss girl named Helene Smith (d. 1929) while in trance spoke Hindustani (Fluornoy, 1900). In 1926 George Valiantine of New York used an old form of Chinese current during the time of Confucius (Bradley, 1924). An English medium, pseudonym 'Rosemary', spoke in an ancient Egyptian idiom dating from the fourteenth century B.C. (Wood, 1955). Teresa Neumann (d. 1962), Bavarian peasant and mystic, spoke the Aramaic vernacular current in the time of Christ (Carty, 1956). More recently, a young woman regressed by Dr Paul Hughes, a psychologist of Montebello, California, spoke ancient Coptic (Cerminara, 1973). Not one of these persons was remotely familiar with the languages they used.

Other occasions of recall probably occur in our dreams, some of which are thought to reveal past events, in actual or symbolical form, and we see ourselves re-enacting some critical situation of our former lives. Dream researchers believe it is possible to cultivate and direct the dream mechanism for the purpose of getting back to the past. We can start doing this by analysing our dreams in detail, noting any unusually vivid scenes that evoke strong emotions in us, as this is taken to indicate that they have a bearing on what happened to us long ago.

Some people have seen what they believe were their own past selves or those of others during out-of-the-body experiences, when they have moved out of the physical body in astral form. The Australian writer G.M. Glaskin describes an interesting method of astral travel he has perfected, which takes place in full consciousness, without recourse to drugs, hypnosis or any apparatus, that enables a person to journey through time and space, to various countries, various periods of history, and at times even to re-experience events of his previous incarnations.

In this method, the experimentee, or person being 'run', or sent off in this manner, lies comfortably on his back, eyes closed, shoes off. Two friends are needed to help in the experiment. One massages the person's ankles, and the other the 'third eye' position or lower centre of the forehead. Various visualization exercises are then carried out by the subject as a result of which astral projection is achieved.

Drugs, especially psychedelic drugs like LSD, also produce a kind of discoincidence, which sometimes brings the user into contact with a sphere reminiscent of an earlier life. Such drugs considerably expand the range of our consciousness but the benefits of this method have been questioned because of the distorting effect of the drugs and the possibly false information they provide.

People with a natural faculty for ESP who are able to dissociate easily from their surroundings, are more likely to establish contact with dimensions that give access to the storehouse of the past. Some claim to achieve this by prolonged auto-suggestion. Psychics of special sensitivity are said to be able to go back in time and view scenes from the panorama of bygone events. While in trance, spiritualist mediums too have occasionally received communications through their controls about the lives of people in their past incarnations.

In answer to a question sometimes put to him about why people do not normally remember the way they have travelled in their previous lives, Rudolf Steiner, (d. 1925) replied, 'The entrance to the path is opened by right meditation.' But meditation is not always easy. It requires months, perhaps years, of practice and discipline before it will yield the secrets of the past. It does not require deep concentration but a kind of mind-wandering, even reverie, which helps to 'unfocus' and at the same time exalt consciousness.

There are other ways too in which one can be helped to remember the past. Certain free-association methods employed in psychoanalysis are believed to be useful. These can provide clues to important incidents in one's earlier lives. Here again, any thoughts that evoke a strong emotional response should be noted and traced to their source by other more deliberate methods.

One such method involves the technique of far-memory training. Starting from the present you systematically review your own life, going back step by step through adolescence to childhood, using as stepping stones only those episodes that you think were turning points in your life. If you persevere you may suddenly find that you have discovered a link to one of your past incarnations. This should then be meditated upon to unfold its full implications.

Another method is to pick out one or more landmarks in your life and analyse the circumstances that led up to them. Try to unravel the purpose behind them and find out why each such incident occurred. Also, study your special skills and aptitudes and see how you acquired them. Or, study your likes and dislikes of people, your phobias and philias with regard to objects and situations, and see if you can account for them. In tracking these indications to their origins the buried incidents of past lives will gradually be exhumed and brought to the surface.

Aleister Crowley (d. 1947), the famous English magician, referred to some of these methods in his *Liber Thisharb* (the word Thisharb is the reverse spelling of the Hebrew phrase B'rashith, 'In the beginning', the first words of the Bible), also called *Liber Viae Memoriae* (The Book of the Path of Memory). These methods were necessary in developing what Crowley called the 'magical memory' that enabled one to recall one's past life. Essentially, one has to remember events in sequence from the present to the past, until, moving back along the time-track one gets to the 'beginning'.

Another method of regressing people to their former lifetimes is known as hypersentience. Here, by means of yogic relaxation exercises, a light trance is induced, during which the subconscious 'memory banks' are stimulated and an expansion of consciousness is brought about. The present personality of the subject, though submerged, remains intact and in control. To start with, the aid of a 'facilitator' or guide is usually required, but as progress is made it becomes possible to make the 'retrotrip' on one's own without the guide's help. The technique is described in a book by Marcia Moore entitled *Hypersentience*. It was as a result of hypersensing that a woman named Barbara Lynne Devlin learned how to go back in time to re-live her previous lives, including her incarnation as Mary Wollstonecraft Shelley, wife of the romantic poet (Devlin, 1977, p.20).

Today the technique most commonly used is age regression under hypnosis, when subjects are directed to go back to their childhood, infancy, prenatality in the foetal period in the womb, and still further back to their previous incarnations. While under hypnosis they allegedly provide information on the language, costume, customs, history, along with names and dates, relating to the period concerned. Sometimes they see themselves in melodramatic situations, perhaps ending in a violent and painful death which they live over with frightening agony.

# 5
# The Case Against Reincarnation

Conclusive proof of reincarnation has so far been impossible to obtain. Although Gina Cerminara states that in her opinion 'within the next fifty years, if not sooner, this proof will be forthcoming' (Cerminara, 1957, p.43), it is difficult to foresee what new manifestations will come to light that will turn the balance decisively in favour of the theory.

To collect and analyse the material and assess the merits of the evidence, assuming this were available, requires the combined qualifications of a psychiatrist, a lawyer, a historian and a detective. Ideally, the observer must be a person of acknowledged competence, well versed in the subject, experienced in investigating this type of phenomena, and careful and deliberate in his observations. The possibility of hallucinations and delusions on the part of the subject, and suppression of facts and tendentious reporting on the part of the observer must always be taken into account.

The psychological attitude of the observer is of paramount importance. He must not be swayed either by antagonism or sympathy. He must not be predisposed by temperament, cultural or family background, education or religion, to believe in the phenomena under observation. Nor must he be predisposed, for the same reasons, to reject the evidence.

As has been noted, the most fashionable method of establishing reincarnation today is to hypnotize a subject and then question him, the material being recorded on tape. That the person is asked to regress to an earlier life already presupposes what the questioner seeks to prove. The presumption of reincarnation is seldom resisted, and leading questions and suggestions by the hypnotist, even if unintentional, further confuse the issue. Today material of this kind is to be had in abundance, with little corroborative data to support it. Often reincarnation is the first and only explanation put forward, and all the evidence built around it. This precludes further rational interpretation and virtually ends the scientific examination of other possibilities.

In seeking for the origins of the belief in reincarnation, psychologists surmise that it may have had its beginnings in the deep human interest in death and life after death, or have arisen from certain primitive explanations concerning dreams and trance states. Also, the remarkable resemblance that some children have to their deceased kinfolk, might suggest that they are the latter born again.

The cultural background of a society often determines the kind of belief that is held about life after death. It has been noted that in countries where reincarnation is part of the religious tradition, many more cases are recorded than elsewhere. According to an international census on the subject taken in 1966, the prevalence of reincarnation incidents was found to be higher in cultures where reincarnation is a matter of general belief, and where cultural attitudes are not opposed to the idea that people are born again into this life, and parents are more likely to accept the claims of children who allegedly remember their past lives.

Most of these cases come from the Hindu and Buddhist countries of southeast Asia where there is a culturally endorsed history of credulity in favour of reincarnation. The Indian investigator, Professor C.T.K. Chari, writing of some cases suggestive of rebirth examined by him says, 'It is disconcerting to learn that out of some 300 alleged cases, over 100 are from India. Can we ignore a cultural predisposition to interpret the facts in accordance with a myth-motif?' (Hick, 1979, p.374).

Other geographical areas are: Lebanon and Syria, where the Druses, a syncretic Moslem sect, believe in the transmigration of souls; Brazil, where the belief is widely held, and is further reinforced by the popular spiritist movement of Allan Kardec (d. 1869); and Alaska, where the Tlingit Indians of the north Pacific coast are traditional believers in a continuing series of lives on earth.

**The Christian View**

Christian scholars are generally agreed that reincarnation is not part of orthodox Christian dogma, although certain passages in the New Testament are sometimes quoted as indicating that it was implicit in the teachings of Christ. These passages, they state, are far from unequivocal, and have been misinterpreted or taken out of context.

In one passage Christ asks his disciples to tell him what others say that he is, and his disciples reply, 'Some say that thou art John the Baptist, some Elias (Elijah), and others Jeremiah or one of the prophets' (Matt. 16.14). This is often quoted as showing that Jesus and his disciples believed in reincarnation. The Christian argument is that since John the Baptist was a contemporary of Jesus and had been beheaded only a few months earlier, there was no suggestion that Jesus was John reincarnated. Again, the Bible says that Elijah did not die but was transported to heaven in a fiery chariot, and the reference is to the miraculous return of Elijah in his actual bodily form to prepare the way for the Messiah (Mal. 4.5). Elijah, as well as Jeremiah and certain other prophets were believed by the Jews of the time not to have died but to be in heaven, helping the Jews, as we find stated, for example, in certain apocryphal works: 'I will send my servants Isaiah and Jeremiah to help you' (2 Esdras, 2.18).

In another passage the disciples ask Jesus about a man born blind from birth: 'Who did sin, this man, or his parents, that he was born blind?' (John 9.2). The answer of Jesus that neither the man nor his parents had sinned would suggest that far from accepting the notion of reincarnation, he rejected it.

In a third passage, when Nicodemus the Pharisee came to Jesus he was told, 'Verily, verily, I say unto thee, except a man be born again, he cannot see the kingdom of God'. To his surprised enquiry of how a man could be born again when he was old, or enter a second time into his mother's womb, Jesus replied, 'Except a man be born of water and of the Spirit, he cannot enter into the kingdom of God' (John 3.5). Rebirth is here specifically explained in terms of spiritual and not bodily rebirth.

Finally, there is a passage in the last book of the New Testament which reads: 'Him that overcometh will I make a pillar in the temple of my God, and he shall go no more out' (Rev. 3.12).

The last phrase is more correctly rendered in the New English Bible, 'and he shall never leave it', which emphasizes the permanence of the final state of blessedness, without any implication of reincarnation on the material plane.

In the religions that accept the idea of reincarnation we find the subject repeatedly dwelt upon in their scriptures, their philosophy and their art. This is not the case with either orthodox Judaism or Christianity (nor, for that matter, with orthodox Islam) and the few ambiguous verses from the Old Testament and the New that are sometimes picked out by those who seek to uphold it cannot be taken as evidence of the doctrine having formed part of the teachings of these religions.

**Reincarnation and the Early Church**

It has sometimes been said, and Dr Leslie Weatherhead has assembled some evidence to support it, that reincarnation was a doctrine to which the early Christian church gave credence, and that it narrowly missed becoming part of orthodox Christianity. But Professor John Hick, who has taught theology at the universities of Cambridge, Birmingham, Cornell and Princeton, and has gone into this matter in some depth points out that Weatherhead 'erroneously and misleadingly' asserts that reincarnation was accepted by the early church (Hick, 1979, p.392).

The facts seem to be that metempsychosis or transmigration was preached by the Gnostics (see page 36) who believed, among other things, that after death human souls could be re-embodied not only in human but also in animal form, and who did a great deal to propagate the idea. The teachings of the *metempsychi*, as they were dubbed, were often quoted by the early church fathers, and as often repudiated, ridiculed and rejected as a fabulous delusion, unworthy of credence, and inadmissable as true doctrine for Christian believers.

The first Christian reference to the transmigration of human souls after death into the bodies of animals, occurs in the writings of Justin Martyr (d. 165), where he mentions the idea, only to turn it down. In spite of this, Wincenty Lutoslawski in his book (1928) lists Justin as a believer in reincarnation.

Irenaeus (d. 202) likewise repudiates the teaching, especially on the ground that we do not recollect our past lives.

Clement of Alexandria (d. 220) accepts the soul's pre-existence, but not on earth, and makes a number of brief references to reincarnation, which he criticizes as primitive and absurd and accordingly rejects.

Tertullian (d. 230) rejected both the Platonic doctrine of pre-existence and the Pythagorean doctrine of repeated existences.

Hippolytus (d. 236) also criticized the doctrine, particularly in the crude and repugnant form presented by the Gnostics. The soul, he stated, comes from God and returns to God.

In the fourth century we find that Lactantius (d. 325), Arnobius (d. 327) and Gregory of Nyssa (d. 395), all condemned 'the heathen teaching of successive incorporation', as did St. Augustine (d. 430) in the fifth century.

It was held by many early Christian thinkers that if the soul was not purified in this life the purification would have to be accomplished in a future life, but not on earth, an idea that was formulated in the concept of purgatory.

St Jerome (d. 420) summarized the situation when he said that the doctrine of reincarnation was taught in the schools along with the arguments against it, so that Christians might be equipped to discuss the matter when it was put forward by those who upheld the teaching.

Origen (d. 254) one of the most learned of the early church fathers is frequently named as one of the chief advocates of reincarnation, but this is also said to be incorrect. What he did write about was pre-existence, and the final return of all things to salvation.

In Origen's view, all souls come from God and all are 'dowered with free will'. Some remain in the paths of righteousness and take the form of angels. Some, still in the exercise of free will, descend to evil and become devils. Human beings have a special relationship with God, but because of the Fall they have suffered an estrangement from the heavenly glory.

All human souls pre-exist in a transearthly realm, but because they are untested and immature they are put through a series of probations. According to the virtues or sins of the soul in that transearthly realm, it is incarnated on earth in fortunate or unfortunate circumstances. While on earth it undergoes another period of testing, and according to its conduct is accorded a place of honour or dishonour in various levels of the spiritu world to work out its further progress.

Origen does not speak of a succession of lives on earth, and in fact he explicitly repudiates the idea of the soul's recurrent return to earth in bodily form.

Origen further proceeds to elaborate on what is known in Greek as *apocatastasis*, 'restitution' or 'restoration', of which there is a hint in the Bible (Acts, 3.21). According to this teaching, God does not desire the death of a sinner, but rather that he should turn from his wickedness and live. Because of divine mercy all creatures will in time return to God, purified, redeemed and perfected. This includes not only the human race, but the demonic hierarchy as well, including Satan himself.

These ideas prevailed for some time among various Christian groups, and it was to combat them that the second Council of Constantinople was convened by the emperor Justinian in A.D. 553. Its censure was directed in particular against the doctrine of pre-existence as taught by the Neoplatonists, and the doctrine of restitution as interpreted by Origen. The Council accordingly decreed: 'If anyone assert the fantastic pre-existence of souls, and shall submit to the monstrous restoration (apocatastasis) that follows it, let him be anathema.'

**Writers and Artists**

More recently, in order to lend support to reincarnation, several compilations have been assembled, of the declarations of great men and women, past and present, including poets, philosophers, novelists and psychologists, among others, expressing their conviction that they have lived before on earth. It should here be noted that often those who believe in the pre-existence and immortality of the soul are quoted as supporting reincarnation, although the two are not identical beliefs. Pre-existence is pre-carnate, and not inter-carnate, existence.

Among the moderns whose words are frequently cited are German writers and thinkers like Lessing, Fichte, Hegel, Schelling and Heine, and British and American poets like Shelley, Browning, Tennyson, Longfellow, Emerson, Whitman and Whittier.

Besides supporting the theory in general terms, some indeed have claimed intuitive or actual experience of their past lives.

The French novelist Gustave Flaubert (d. 1880) wrote, 'Sometimes I see myself quite clearly in the different ages of history, and I have memories of engaging in different trades and experiencing various fortunes'.

The Finnish composer Jean Sibelius (d. 1957) said, 'Millions of years ago, in my previous incarnations, I must have been related to swans or wild geese, because I can still feel that affinity'.

Salvador Dali (born 1904) Spanish surrealist painter declared that he could remember vividly his previous life as the Spanish mystic St. John of the Cross (d. 1591), and his fellow monks, and the monastery where they lived. He adds, 'I can remember experiencing the divine union, and of understanding the dark night of the soul of which St John writes with so much feeling' (Iverson, 1977, p.144).

Many of these opinions can as easily be ascribed to the artistic, musical or literary temperament, and a soaring imagination that feels an intimacy with the great personages of the past, and even a kinship with the animal kingdom and all creation. An equally impressive anthology could be compiled quoting eminent personalities, including many who have given their endorsement to the theory of rebirth, expressing contrary views, and discounting reincarnation and all it implies.

The extent of a poet's licence or an artist's reverie is not to be bound by a passing and perhaps fanciful notion that he had existed in an earlier time. The thoughts of such a person will cover a wide range of views on many and varied subjects, not always consistent, and not necessarily representing a firmly held belief.

The thought that they may have lived before, and that there is a possibility that they might return again, is one that has at some time or other flashed momentarily across the minds of many thinking persons, and they may have sometimes toyed with the idea and given expression to it, without seriously advancing it as representing their deep convictions or adopting it as a philosophy of life.

Critics therefore point out that the testimony provided by famous people on a subject of this nature, interesting though it is, hardly establishes reincarnation as a reality, and their intuitions, however rhetorically expressed, do not constitute evidence.

Writers and artists have been known to get so emotionally

involved with their work as to identify with their creations. The dramatist who holds long conversations with the imaginary protagonists of his plays, the novelist who gets sick when describing the poisoning of his fictional heroine, are examples of the extraordinary empathizing power of the creative imagination. The Canadian opera singer, Don Garrard, believes that he has lived in the past as a Russian monk, a Roman centurion, a French courtier, among others, but significantly, while he is singing the relevant operatic part. He says of his Egyptian incarnation, 'When I sing Ramphis, the Egyptian high priest in Verdi's *Aida*, I know that I lived as a high priest in Egypt, about 4000 years B.C. (Underwood and Wilder, 1975, p.181).

**Group Reincarnation**

In the preceding chapters we have already examined in some detail the actual evidence provided in some recent cases of claimed reincarnation which have been seriously investigated. We have also shown that researchers have put forward alternative explanations that do not require the hypothesis of a past life on earth. Even the evidence produced by Dr Ian Stevenson and other investigators of high standing can strictly be regarded as little more than anecdotal. It is simply beyond positive proof or confirmation and must in the end remain a matter of speculation.

The case for reincarnation finds fewer exponents when the possibility is suggested that a number of people who have lived through and shared in a period of intense emotional or spiritual crisis, would thereafter tend to reincarnate together in another era.

Such reincarnation is said to be due to collective or national karma, in which groups, or indeed whole communities, move in collective soul-cycles. Karma, it is said, applies not only to individuals but extends to families, tribal groups, races, and nations. This is so because they all follow the same spiritual destiny, or are involved in the same group experience, and participate in the same surge of spiritual evolution. Sometimes such groups of people are said to reincarnate collectively to fulfil a common task, reconcile some incomplete issue, or purge themselves of a collective sin.

Edgar Cayce believed that the souls of all those involved in the cruel conquistador invasions of Mexico under Hernando

Cortés (d. 1547), and of Peru under Francisco Pizarro (d. 1541), were in due time reincarnated *en masse* in twentieth-century Spain to be caught up in the terrible fratricidal civil war and involved in the carnage, and in this manner expiated the sins of their past. He also stated that the sufferings of the Jews under the Nazis were definitely a karmic result of their cruelty and ruthlessness as a racial group centuries ago (Cerminara, 1973, p.144).

Perhaps the foremost exponent of collective reincarnation today is Dr Arthur Guirdham, who traces the lives of a particular group of people through their various incarnations in such books as *We Are One Another* (1974), and *The Lake and the Castle* (1976) involving characters with whom Guirdham claims to have been closely associated for two thousand years.

In the latter book he tabulates the various names of these individuals as they appeared in Rome in the fourth century A.D.; in Celtic Christian Cumberland in the seventh century; in Languedoc, France, in the thirteenth century; in Napoleonic France in the eighteenth century; and finally in our own times. The facility with which Dr Guirdham speaks of 'my Roman incarnation', 'her Celtic period', 'his Napoleonic life', makes such a tabulation necessary, as otherwise it would be difficult to keep track of the numerous metamorphoses of his *dramatis personae*.

While Dr Guirdham has furnished us with descriptions of the group members and recounts the events of their past and present lives in great detail, we are not in a position to verify them direct from these sources. These contemporary associates of Dr Guirdham's, about twelve in number, from whom some supplementary data might have been obtained, all unfortunately died between 1969 and 1973 of coronary attack, angina pectoris, cancer, apoplexy and so on, so that we are unable to obtain any corroborative evidence that would give some measure of scientific endorsement to his record. One cannot help feeling that Dr Guirdham was perhaps too deeply involved with his vast project, and that his 'epic of verification', as he calls it, would have benefitted from the supporting testimony of an impartial outside investigator of the calibre of Dr Ian Stevenson.

It has been noted that for some people it could be a matter of pride to be accounted members of a tenacious group soul so that they could boast of the multiplicity of their incarnations, 'almost as if some sort of Olympic championship were involved' (Langley, 1967, p.21). But group rebirth is only one of the stumbling blocks in the way of a wider acceptance of the theory of reincarnation. Further problems arise in considering some other questions.

What are we to say, for instance, to those who assert that people can not only be regressed to the past, but 'ongressed' to the future? How can two contemporaries both have lived in the past as Joan of Arc? How seriously can we take the stories of those who remember having lived in Atlantis in 12,000 B.C., on the moon 600,000 years ago, and on a planet with a name something like Anaminta in the Andromeda galaxy 72 million years ago (Devlin, 1977, p.235). Such claims have been the subject of much unflattering comment and have strained to breaking point the faith of even many confirmed believers who would otherwise be prepared to look at all the evidence through enchanted glasses.

And what are we to say of the historical-biographical novels based on true memories of former lives? At best they must remain fictional. P.D. Ouspensky (d. 1947), Russian mystic and pupil of Gurdjieff, remarked, 'Very often you hear people say, chiefly in connection with what they call "reincarnation", that they can remember their lives in previous incarnations, and they write books about what they were before. This is pure fantasy.'

The information in such novels, though sometimes of great interest, is for the most part trivial and hardly worth the effort of following up, and few historians would take such accounts seriously. And as for the unsupported and often absurdly far-fetched claims of those at a lesser remove, unkind critics will point out that our mental hospitals are filled with people re-living their lives as Cleopatra and Napoleon.

### Underlying Motivations

To take the most uncompromising position, the evidence in any instance may be dismissed as a hoax perpetrated by the person claiming the experience of a past incarnation. Here we may have an individual, neglected and unfulfilled, who desires the limelight, and craves some small measure of publicity so that he might enjoy the fame, however transient, of belonging to the select band of 'those who have lived before'.

Even if deception can safely be eliminated, and ignoring the scores of phoney cases that bring the whole discussion into ridicule, there is the possibility of unconscious fraud, a form of self-delusion on the part of the subject who lets his imagination run away with him and unwittingly exaggerates an experience that has perhaps a much more prosaic explanation. Conscious or unconscious, the motivation of fraud may be wishful thinking, or escapism, so that a person leading a humdrum life might want to regress to a more glamorous past, to live life with grand-opera themes and become caliph for an hour. His unconscious tells him, 'This clerical job is a bore, but in the days when I was Mark Antony ...'.

The famous physical medium Daniel Dunglas Home (d. 1886), himself the object of one of Robert Browning's barbed shafts, wrote, 'I have had the pleasure of meeting at least twelve Marie Antoinettes, six or seven Marys of Scotland, a whole host of Louis and other kings, about twenty Great Alexanders, but never a plain John Smith. I, indeed, would like to cage the latter curiosity.'

Although persistent jibes of this kind have resulted in recent claimants giving more modest accounts of their past lives, the general criticism remains unaltered.

Analysis of the motivations underlying certain reincarnation claims, has led in some cases to an explanation in terms of pathological disorders. It is well known that physical or mental illness lowers the normal barrier between the everyday world and the other dimension. According to Pythagorean belief, the soul often develops psychic powers during bodily sickness. Plato said that the prophetic spirit is more likely to manifest itself when the body is distraught by disease. Sickness, it would seem, facilitates genuine paranormal perception, including a higher level of psychic sensitivity. At the same time the imaginative faculty may be greatly enhanced.

One of the strange mental conditions about which a great deal has still to be learned is epilepsy, a group of diseases of the central nervous system, whose symptoms include the sudden impairment or complete loss of consciousness. According to the ancients the utterances of prophets, sibyls and diviners were often characterized by a seizure very much like that of epilepsy.

The Greeks called epilepsy the 'sacred disease', believing that during an attack the victim became the mouthpiece of the gods, who spoke through him.

It is curious that before the onset of an attack the victim may have a premonition of its coming, and in some cases feels that some great mystery is about to be revealed to him. Epileptic symptoms may include speaking in a strange voice, or in some foreign or unknown language (xenoglossis). There is often a feeling of semitrance or dreaminesss during which the patient imagines that he is in some place that is new and yet strangely familiar (déjàism). Scenes from his early childhood drift into his mind, and he may even feel that he is transported back to another time altogether. Dr Guirdham points out that epileptic reactions in an adolescent can indicate the latter's capacity to 'step out of time', and adds that déjàism is 'common among epileptics'.

Another mental condition that has been suggested as a possible causative factor in a great many reincarnation claims is hysteria. Although once associated with young women, this is an affliction to which both men and women, young and old, can be subject. It is not an organic disease, that is, it is not caused by damage to the body, but a functional disorder.

Among its many symptoms or manifestations are: hyperaesthesia, or excessive acuteness of the senses; hallucinations, both visual and auditory; the creation of imaginary characters with whom conversations are held; depersonalization, in which the individual loses his or her sense of personal identity; personation, where factual information about other people, gained either direct or through ESP, is enacted in dramatic form; and dissociation, or a shifting of the personality. Psychologists point out that the personalities, different from our own, that emerge, either spontaneously in hysteria or under hypnosis or other trance states, are dissociated portions of ourselves.

Hysterical stigmata are not unknown, where a person's body will take on marks, wounds or scars that cannot be accounted for in physical terms. The hysteric, during his period of hysteria, can become a superb actor, and his inventiveness (mythomania, as it is called) is often astonishing. A hysterical subject does not always, and indeed cannot always distinguish between fact and fancy, between reality and his own inventions. The eminent physician Sir Francis Walshe described the hysteric as an actor who becomes more and more convinced by his own acting, and 'may, ultimately, come and join the audience'. Hysterics can act, play, mimic and behave out of their normal character quite naturally, without the least effort.

It is medically established that cerebral malfunction, from whatever cause, can give rise to dissociated states and at times lead to the illusion that one is somewhere else, or is experiencing something else, or has had an experience before. We know that the two hemispheres of the brain function as a unit because of a bundle of nerve fibres (the corpus callosum) that connects them. Injury to these nerve fibres, or a momentary malfunctioning for whatever reason, can inhibit the normal correlation of the two separate halves and result in dual time-and-place perception. Thus, the independent perception of the two hemispheres with one lagging behind the other could produce the sensation of elapsed time. In such cases even if the time separation is only a fraction of a second, the subject could experience something and then experience it again a split second later, leaving him with the feeling that he has already experienced it long before, as in déjàism.

Similarly, the persistent illusion that a subject might have of having lived before, is regarded by some psychologists as indicating a mental aberration of some kind. This could have a largely physical origin, reinforced perhaps by hysteric tendencies. For this reason some authorities tend to believe that people who imagine they have lived in a previous incarnation must either be emotionally disturbed or mentally ill.

Dr Ian Stevenson, an extremely cautious observer, stated that three out of his eighteen subjects did develop clinical mental illness in later life.

### The Second Body and Possession

Hysteria, epilepsy and other mental afflictions are among the many conditions that are conducive to xenophrenic or 'strange-minded' states, when the conscious mind is partially or totally in abeyance. This is still a virtually unexplored area of psychological enquiry. In occult terms, when the waking adult is functioning at the practical level the Second Body (the astral and etheric double) and the physical body are in perfect alignment or 'coincidence'. In xenophrenia there is a greater or lesser degree of 'discoincidence' in the alignment of the two bodies, and this displacement results in an alteration of consciousness. The firm grip of the conscious mind is relaxed and influences from the unconscious rise to the surface.

Also, through the crack or chink between the two dissociated bodies material from the supra-physical planes may intrude, providing experiences of other dimensions. The 'mind' of the Second Body is independent of the physical brain through which the conscious mind normally operates. Geniuses are thought to be in slight discoincidence during their creative moments. William Blake (d. 1827), poet and mystic, was said to be 'cracked' but, as Edith Sitwell commented, 'that was where the light came through'.

Xenophrenia is also present in all trance and semi-trance situations, as when a person is under the influence of drugs or alcohol, during sleep, under hypnosis, in times of acute mental stress, physical illness, depression, intense emotion.

In certain trance conditions the Second Body is believed to separate from the physical body, resulting in the phenomenon variously known as astral projection, out-of-the-body (OOB) experience, or exteriorization. At such times it may lift off and move into a different plane, that is, into another time-and-place dimension. The accounts of people who have had such experiences and remembered them afterwards suggest that the astral body can translate itself in a flash to some other part of the earth's surface, or observe scenes from the historical past, or visit the spirit world (Walker, 1974).

The astral body will not always be seen or heard by those among whom it finds itself. In any event, such OOB experience could be advanced to account for certain reincarnation episodes. Edgar Cayce, for instance, said that during his self-induced trance his astral body would become dissociated from his physical body so that he could move at will from one plane of consciousness to another. Edward Ryall (see page 71) said that he was sometimes 'transported' to the scenes of his past life. From the occult point of view some reincarnation experiences could be explained in terms of some such astral adventure.

Some people, occultists and spiritualists among them, advance the theory of possession as another possibility. Possession is the apparent taking over of a person's mind and body by some intruding discarnate entity. This is not the same as mediumistic trance, when the spirit of a dead person makes temporary use of the medium's physical apparatus and speaks through her. In possession, the subject's mind is apparently displaced, and he falls under the dominance of the discarnate personality.

In this view, subjects who claim to remember their past incarnations may be possessed by an earth-bound entity who has lived before. It is said that earth-bound spirits are particularly liable to possess living beings. Such possessing (expersonating) spirits choose particular victims because they are easy to get at: the feeble-minded, the insane, the sensual, the morally depraved, the drug addict, the drunkard, those in deep depression or in any state of xenophrenia or strange-mindedness as in hypnotic trance. Also those whose defences are lowered due to weakened health.

For various reasons earth-bound souls have failed to develop properly. They cannot or will not migrate like other souls to the different spiritual realms for their further evolution after the demise of the body, but remain in the vicinity of their earthly life. Often they may not even realize that they are no longer physically alive, but are actually dead; or knowing they are dead they may be terrified of the new life in the unknown; they may be unwilling to leave the old earthly haunts with which they are familiar. Frequently they are bound by some blinding passion, like love, hatred, jealousy, revenge, remorse, to a particular habitation or person. Again, a sense of frustration, fear, panic or other overwhelming emotion would keep such a spirit in a condition of semi-insanity, creating an uncontrollable desire to return to physical form.

### The Spiritualist View

Spiritualists are divided on the subject of reincarnation, the majority repudiating the doctrine entirely. The great Swedish mystic and scholar, Emanuel Swedenborg (d. 1772), who has been referred to as the 'first spiritualist', claimed that he had visited heaven and hell and conversed with the souls of the dead, and brought back much information of this world and the next. Every man, he declared, is a new creation, and has never existed on earth before. Recollection of past lives, where claims of such are put forward, are deceits projected by Satan and his minions, devils and evil spirits, into the minds of those susceptible to receive such illusions. Belief in reincarnation, he said, was dangerous, since it made the mind receptive to false notions provided by lying spirits, and adversely affected the progress of the soul and its advance to heaven.

The most important offshoot of the spiritualist movement favouring the doctrine of reincarnation is spiritism, founded by the French writer Allan Kardec (d. 1869). But it is said that an entity, speaking through the famous Scots medium D.D. Home in 1869 shortly after Kardec's death and claiming to be Kardec himself, expressed regret at having taught the spiritist doctrine and propagating the idea of reincarnation.

The author and pioneer English spiritualist, William Howitt (d. 1879) who wrote about the religious and philosophical aspects of spiritualism, and whom Charles Dickens consulted about haunted houses, called the reincarnationist doctrine, 'pitiable and repellent'.

Spiritualist evidence ostensibly confirms that Madame Blavatsky (d. 1891), like Kardec, made a posthumous recantation. In her post-mortem existence she realised that her advocacy of reincarnation was misguided, and that she had taught erroneous doctrines, and was now working to get herself and her victims free.

The mystic, clairvoyant and trance healer, Andrew Jackson Davis (d. 1910), also known as the 'Poughkeepsie Seer' after his home town in New York State, allegedly received many spirit communications from the next world, and asserted categorically that the doctrine of reincarnation was 'a magnificent mansion built on sand'.

The spiritualist J.J. Morse (d. 1919), a trance medium through whom certain bygone personalities are believed to have sent inspirational and factual messages, declared that he had received several communications stating that 'reincarnation was nonsense', and warning against it.

Dr Carl A. Wickland (*c.* 1924) of the Psychopathic Institute of Chicago, and member of the American Association for the Advancement of Science, who devoted his life to the subject of after-death experiences, spirit possession, insanity and obsessions, was another opponent. In his findings, published in 1924, he wrote that those who die convinced that they will be reincarnated, carry this conviction with them into the next world, imagine that they must return to another earth life, become befuddled and hold up their own further evolution. The belief was not only false but harmful, for it acted as a psychic barrier and impeded progress to the higher spiritual planes after death. Dr Wickland and his wife in their contact with earth-bound spirits who caused obsessions in the living, found that many of these spirits had been Theosophists in their lifetime and had believed in reincarnation.

Even today critics point out that people who believe they are reincarnated carry the memory of their past as a terrible burden that slows down their maturity as individuals. Stevenson found that in some cases preoccupation with past memories interfered with adaptation to present life conditions. He states that in several cases where a previous personality had committed suicide, the present subject showed an inclination to contemplate suicide, and one of them actually did put an end to his own life.

Spiritualists assert that the phenomena associated with regression events have been duplicated in the seance room. Mediums in trance sometimes dramatically assume the voice and character of the controlling spirit; they alter in facial appearance and affect a different form of speech. The kind of historical data obtained from so-called reincarnated personalities has been obtained through mediums from spirits. A person regressed under hypnosis may be able to make contact with the other side, operating as a medium with or without the aid of a spirit guide. Some of the facts, including names of people and places, provided by spirits through automatic writing or other means have been confirmed from parish registers and other documentary sources (Manning, 1978).

Much of the material recorded by Dr Arthur Guirdham, perhaps the most articulate recent exponent of reincarnation, was by his own admission received from discarnate personalities and revenants or returning spirits, so the question of what came to him by personal experience of the past and what through spirit entities is not clear.

Spiritualists say that no theory of reincarnation is required to explain other supernormal phenomena. Déjàism may represent a transient brush with the spirit of a person who has lived in a certain place before. The feats of calculators and other child prodigies may represent a form of temporary possession. Xenoglossis is explicable in terms of mind-tapping, or the recrudescence of an ancestral memory, or it may be a communication from the dead, where one is only the mouthpiece of a spirit. And as for historical novels and other literary works, spiritualist archives are bulging with such material received through mediumship.

**Pearl Curran and 'Patience Worth'**

One of the best known cases of this kind is that of Mrs Pearl Curran (d. 1937), of St Louis, Missouri, who was herself not particularly well read, nor had she any literary friends or associates. In the course of five years she received through a spirit entity named 'Patience Worth' a series of novels and poems of quite prodigious literary quality totalling in all over one and a half million words.

One of these novels was described by Dr Usher, professor of history at the University of Washington, as 'the greatest story penned of the life and times of Christ since the Gospels were finished'. Another novel about mid-Victorian English Society was hailed by the *New York Herald Tribune* as 'a work approximating absolute genius'. There was also a poem on medieval England, some 65,000 words in length, 90 per cent of them pure Anglo-Saxon, speaking of which Professor F.C.S. Schiller (d. 1937) British philosopher who taught at Oxford, could only say, 'We are face to face with a philological miracle'. Professor Allison of Manitoba University regarded the Patience Worth case as 'the outstanding phenomenon of the age'.

The 1918 American anthology of the year's best poems carried three poems by Amy Lowell (d. 1925), Imagist poet and biographer of Keats; three poems by Vachel Lindsay (d. 1931); two by Sara Teasdale (d. 1933); one by Edgar Lee Masters (d. 1950), all American poets well known in their day. There were also five by Patience Worth. The National Arts Club of New York named her as one of the 'outstanding authors of the year'; and the Joint Committee of Literary Arts of New York recognized her as 'an outstanding novelist'. Yet 'Patience Worth' was not a living person, perhaps had never lived at all, and was the unconscious, subconscious, or superconscious creation of an 'untravelled housewife of limited education' (see Yost, 1916; Prince, 1929; Harlow, 1961).

The reincarnation argument on grounds of exceptional talent and precocity has also been countered on many points. To start with, precocity is rarely a lifelong possession. Often the powers fluctuate, and generally decline in later life. The precocious child, it is said, may be picking the brains of others and tapping their store of knowledge.

Precocity is sometimes associated with a physical defect, a disability or peculiarity of some kind. Precocious children may be far from clever in an overall sense. Not infrequently, except in the one direction in which they excel, they are dull-witted and slow of comprehension. Literally scores of *idiots-savants* are on record in various branches of achievement.

The general lack of intelligence is found more especially in the case of prodigy calculators, children or young persons who perform the most extraordinary mathematical feats with remarkable speed. Yet many calculators have been illiterate and mentally undeveloped. Some said that their answers simply came to them or were whispered to them. For this reason either telepathic mind-tapping or possession by discarnate entities have been suggested as possible explanations.

In the case of great geniuses or men of exceptional talent in certain spheres of achievement, special factors seem to be in operation that probably account for their unusual gifts. It has been said that biologically geniuses are like mutants among men, as man is a mutant among animals. Heredity appears to play a part in the incidence of genius. The Bernouilli family in three generations produced eight mathematicians of repute. The heredity factor is probably also present in the case of the Bach family, the Mozart family, the Macaulays, the Darwins, the Huxleys. Some psychologists invoke the yet unplumbed depths of the unconscious mind, which in all probability draws on ranges of knowledge far beyond our awareness.

The great geniuses of the world have never claimed that they received their gifts as a result of their exertions in a past incarnation, nor have any of their biographers made such a claim on their behalf.

### The Power of Suggestion

In any consideration of sociological phenomena the importance of suggestion as a contributing factor to the genesis and spread of ideas cannot be ignored. European history records several episodes of mass sociopathic delirium, such as the dancing mania of Germany (eleventh century); the flagellants, also of Germany (fourteenth century); the witchcraft craze, which first started in Europe (fifteenth to seventeenth centuries), and then spread to America, especially Salem (seventeenth century); the tulipomania of Holland (*c.* 1650); the convulsionaries of France (*c.* 1730); the South Sea Bubble of England (1721). To these may be added the hysteria of modern religious revivals, gold rushes, sporting events, and pop festivals.

There are always people eager to keep abreast of what is going on, some motivated by the desire to learn, some out of curiosity, and some simply in order that they might not be thought old fashioned and out of the mainstream of current events by not following the latest trends. Hence the evidence of mass anxiety that sometimes marks radical changes in fashion, in art and music, in political and religious belief.

The factor that contributed primarily to the widespread interest in reincarnation in the western world, was perhaps the founding of the Theosophical Society in 1875, and the very effective literature they produced on the subject, which for the first time presented to the western public some of the basic teachings underlying eastern religious thought, reincarnation among them. A perusal of any competent history of this extraordinary movement will show that a form of mild mass hysteria took place by slow epidemic spread among certain classes of western society.

Since then curiosity about reincarnation was sustained through the work of men like Edgar Cayce and the books written about him, followed by Morey Bernstein's book *The Search for Bridey Murphy*, which created a fresh upsurge of interest in the subject, and popularized that great standby of the instant reincarnationist – hypnotic age-regression. Parlour hypnotists all over the western world were sending people back to re-live their lives as American Indians, Viking warriors, Moroccan dancing girls, Civil War heroes, Persian satraps, Chinese princesses, Norse berserkers and Arab sheikhs. Such unconscious recall is to be distinguished from the spontaneous, conscious recall of eastern subjects, and may represent an entirely different phenomenon.

What really accelerated the advance of the reincarnation faith was the apparent success of these age-regression experiments, in which a hypnotized subject was made to go back to his childhood and infancy, not a difficult performance, and then still further back to an apparent life before the present one. Sometimes he was even made to re-enact episodes of this past life, like a patient abreacting during psychoanalytic treatment. This success was due in large measure to the fact that the means used, hypnosis, is itself one of the most effective methods of achieving suggestibility, including hallucinations, in subjects, and is therefore to be regarded, according to the experts, as highly dubious.

It has already been pointed out that, to begin with, both the operator and the subject who use hypnosis for age regression, are predisposed to believe in reincarnation, and what they come up with must therefore be accepted with caution. Again, an element of hysteria may be present in a subject who slips easily into a 'past' life and enacts an earlier incarnation in dramatic fashion. Age regression satisfies the subject's unconscious desire to create and live out an imaginary past which is made up to be more like what he thinks his past ought to have been.

Even in the absence of hysterical fantasizing, it is to be remembered, that the hypnotized person is in rapport with his hypnotist, and will respond to his suggestions, which at times amount to actual directions, given to him. Hypnotists desirous of establishing their case often ask leading questions, and in other ways mastermind the operation. In these circumstances, the subject is keen to live up to the expectation of what he believes the hypnotist wants to hear or expects from him. He desires to please the operator, and knowing that evidence of regression is sought, regresses to oblige. The process is not less questionable because it may be unconscious.

In her book *Life Before Life*, an American psychologist, Dr Helen Wambach, summarizes the pre-birth experiences of 750 subjects whom she hypnotized, sometimes in mass sessions with over fifty people at a time. As a result of her hypnotic instructions they were induced to take the trip back into what she unequivocally calls 'the time just before you were born into your current lifetime'. Here reincarnation is taken for granted, and the premiss is further reinforced by such loaded questions as: Did you choose to be born? Why did you choose the twentieth century? Did you choose your sex? Did you know your mother-to-be and did you choose her? If, as Dr Wambach suggests, 'the time has come to study rigorously the plausibility of reincarnation', the study will surely not be advanced by experiments of this nature, however 'scientifically' disguised with statistics.

The tendency of the subject to fall in line with the hypnotist's predilections is increased by the fact that there exists what psychologists call a transferential relationship between the two parties involved. Such a relationship is found between analyst and patient, between hypnotist and subject, between guru and chela, between teacher and pupil, when the latter in all these cases often seeks to gain the former's favour, and is prepared to subordinate his personality and will in order to ingratiate himself with the former.

Thus the subject is anxious to gain the esteem of the hypnotist and will adopt a line that will please him. The fact that he is in a trance does not alter, and indeed often strengthens, this relationship. Hence the number of willing subjects who go under and then start inventing their past selves. The role thus unconsciously assumed is often played out with striking histrionic ability.

Confirmation of the directable nature of hypnosis is found in the more objective sphere of experiments conducted in Soviet Russia. In their book on psychic studies that are taking place behind the Iron Curtain, Ostrander and Schroeder relate the experiments of Dr Vladimir L. Raikov in Moscow. He hypnotizes subjects and suggests that they are someone in the past. The subjects are chosen from among students between their later teens and early twenties, and are given between five and twenty reincarnation experiences each. Thus, a student with no natural artistic ability, when converted into Raphael, the famous Florentine painter, begins to show remarkable painting ability after a few sessions, and cannot believe that she has actually painted the pictures before her. The learning process is likewise accelerated in the student who is 'reincarnated' as Fritz Kreisler, the Austrian violinist, or as a famous European mathematical genius. The student 'reincarnated' as a king or queen employs imperious gestures and gives royal commands. The scenes enacted during these 'artificial reincarnation' sessions bear all the marks of verisimilitude.

In this process of reincarnation hypnosis, or active trance, there is no suggestion that the subjects have actually reverted to their own past lives, and hence no hypothesis of reincarnation is put forward. It is taken for what it is. A delusion. A hallucination. A fanciful reconstruction, with no mystical or religious overtones attached.

# 6
# Mind and Memory

The mind is the most extraordinary element that has emerged from the whole evolutionary process. It is a mysterious and still virtually uncharted territory, and we are far from understanding its ultimate nature.

Psychologists are well aware that we have only just begun to scratch the surface of the mind's full potentialities. Against the background of our current knowledge, paltry as it is, they state that the conscious mind, on which we lay such emphasis, is only one layer in a vast and complex spectrum of the mind as a whole. Or, to put it another way, it represents but the tip of an iceberg of himalayan proportions. Beneath, is a huge submerged continent, individual and collective, about which we know almost nothing.

We are unable to explain the emergence of mind from insentient matter during the evolutionary process, unless we presuppose a mental element in inanimate things. We do not know what kind of mind abides in plants or in the lower animals. We do not know at what point in the history of our planet and in what manner, the efflorescence of the human as distinct from the animal mind took place.

We are still ignorant of the full extent of our own individual minds. Thought itself, as commonplace as breathing, is a huge magical creation appearing seemingly out of nowhere. We cannot provide a rational explanation for multiple personality or 'possession', for ecstatic or visionary states, for inspiration, or even for sleep and dreams. As Dr Gustav Eckstein has said, 'Eighty sleep theories have come and gone' (1971, p.708).

We cannot explain the faculty of paraperception, as revealed in the phenomena of ESP and its variants, thought-reading, telepathy, clairvoyance, clairaudience, precognition. Unless we assume that thought is a material force or find a point of contact between thinking and things, we cannot explain how mind can affect matter, as we find in psychosomatics, telekinesis, poltergeist activity, thought photography.

The elusive area where thoughts and things, or mind and body, meet, has been the subject both of philosophical speculation and scientific enquiry for over two thousand years. The problem goes back to our origins and has a wide bearing on the questions arising from reincarnation.

**Evolution and Inheritance**

The physical characteristics that distinguish us as individuals, racial groups and species, are transmitted to us by our progenitors. We retain certain vestiges of our animal past in some of our bodily structures. The coccyx (tail-bone), the scalp and ear muscles, the appendix, and various other vestiges are said to go back to our marine, reptilian and mammalian beginnings. In the embryonic stage of our development within the womb we all recapitulate these early stages of our evolutionary past.

In addition to our animal origins, genetic studies reveal the inheritance of a wide diversity of physical characteristics arising from our parental, ancestral and racial origin. These include bone structure, height, cranial size, shape of nose, skin and hair colour, gait, stance, gesture, health, predisposition to certain diseases, and even bodily marks.

No one knows what causes the birthmarks, dimples, warts and moles (naevi) that we are born with, but it is established that these are often transmitted by our progenitors. Dermatologists and geneticists who have studied the incidence and location of moles in families find that a tendency to have many or fewer moles as well as their location on the body may be inherited (Cockayne, 1933).

The possibility of other bodily marks being brought into existence purely by the moulding power of the mind is also to be taken into account. In mysticism it is noted that a strong belief, a sense of mystical identity, intense contemplation, may lead to the appearance of some physical token of identification between devotee and deity, as we find in the appearance of stigmata or the marks of the crucifixion on the bodies of certain Christian saints.

There is also some evidence of what is called 'maternal psychokinesis', where the thoughts of a pregnant woman may influence the tissues, especially the skin tissues, of the baby in her womb. The fact that a woman has been told that someone is going to be reborn to her, especially if she belongs to a culture where belief in reincarnation is prevalent, may be sufficient to affect the foetus in her womb and produce the corroborative mark. In his investigation of the Tlingit fisherman named William George (see page 81), Dr Ian Stevenson observed that the moles of the deceased fisherman appeared in the identical places on the body of his grandson.

Similarly, strong emotions for the loss of a loved one can create a situation where some bodily tokens of the loved one appear in the later progeny. Thus there is the case of Dr Carmelo Samona, a well-known physician of Palermo, Sicily, whose five-year old daughter, Alexandrina, died of meningitis on 15 March 1910. The mother, Adela Samona, was utterly distraught at the loss, until three days later when Alexandrina appeared to her in a dream and told her not to mourn because she would return to her as another child. Still later, the girl's spirit came through a medium saying that she would be born again as one of twin girls. On 22 November of the same year Señora Samona gave birth to twins, and one of them turned out to be exactly like the dead girl in appearance and personality, with marks on the face like those on Alexandrina's (Hunt, 1964, p.75).

Opponents of the reincarnation hypothesis point out that we all have birthmarks, moles or other blemishes or beauty spots on our bodies, sometimes perhaps even in the same place as a deceased relative, but this does not constitute proof of reincarnation.

Not only moles but even scars received during the lifetime of a person may, it is thought, be transmitted to a child by the power of psychological suggestion. Researchers into reincarnation cases have found people who bore 'sympathy scars' which were claimed to be relics of injuries suffered in the previous life. Guirdham states that he has seen a lesion on a woman's back 'which dates unmistakably from her being struck by a flaming torch on her way to the stake seven centuries previously' (1978, p.21). It is questionable whether this extraordinary claim would find many believers.

In any event, if reincarnation is a matter of the soul and not of the body, the whole argument from moles and scars in discussing reincarnation, becomes irrelevant.

**Memory**

The subject of the transmission of parental and ancestral physical characteristics is further linked with the question of the possible inheritance of parental and ancestral memories. One of the most curious features of the mind is memory, about which we know as little as we do about the mind in general. Memory remains one of the great enigmas of psychology. What is memory? In what part of the brain is it stored? How is it stored? Why do we forget? A famous American brain researcher Dr Karl Lashley spent the greater part of his career trying to locate the place in the brain where the memory might reside. Unsuccessful, he was moved to say in despair that from the evidence of his researches learning ought to be impossible, since there appears to be no physiological explanation of how we remember what we learn.

Yet memory provides us with the ultimate clue to our individual identity, to our personal continuity through periods of unconsciousness such as sleep, to our relationship with the people around us and to our environment. Without memory we would fail to function at all. Memory helps us to retain, recall and recognize experience.

We all possess a rich treasury of memories, although most of it is not at our free disposal. We remain oblivious of huge areas of our racial and ancestral past. We recall only a small fraction of what we experience when we are asleep or otherwise unconscious. We do not even remember, without prompting, most of the incidents of our adult waking lives. Much of what happened to us only a few months ago, still more of what happened to us in childhood, and practically all that occurred in our infancy is forgotten.

Some memories flash suddenly and spontaneously to consciousness, sparked by some chance trigger, a name, a sound, a smell, a glimpse of something associated with the original situation, which then releases a flood of reminiscence. Marcel Proust (d. 1922), psychological novelist, tells how the taste of a little tea-cake sent the mind fleeting back to a host of forgotten incidents of the past.

Certain forms of recall involve what is known as hypermnesia or super-remembering, an exaltation of memory, as it were, during which things are remembered very vividly and in the greatest detail. Such memories most frequently rise to the surface during physical illness, in high fever, in religious exaltation, ecstatic and high emotional conditions, pre-mortem delirium, hysteria, senility, epilepsy, and other xenophrenic or abnormal states of mind.

It has been said that a drowning man sees certain events of his past life flash by in an almost instantaneous panorama of vivid recall. People who have survived falls from a great height also confirm having had the same experience while falling. The famous psychologist and physician Cesare Lombroso (d. 1909) wrote that when he was afflicted with intestinal poisoning one night, certain disagreeable memories of many years ago came back to him with ghastly precision, and with details far more minute and exact than he could possibly have recaptured when in the normal state.

Memories may be revived and reassembled in jumbled or symbolic form in our dreams. Most of the material thus received drifts away and is lost to conscious awareness, but when it comes to what Louis Pasteur (d. 1895) calls 'the prepared mind', it can be put to good use. It can then be combined with information we already possess and can help in our practical problems.

Professor Jean Agassiz (d. 1873), the Swiss naturalist, had a succession of three vivid dreams which filled in all the missing details in an indistinct impression of a fossil fish on a stone slab he had been working on. As a result he was able to restore the complete picture perfectly. Dr Hermann Hilprecht, the Babylonian scholar, puzzling for many months over an undecipherable inscription on some excavated fragments of agate, dreamed one night in 1893 that he was visited by a 'tall thin priest of ancient Nippur', who explained to him the precise arrangement of the inscription, and thus opened the way to its correct decipherment and meaning.

Recollection of the buried past can sometimes be stimulated by alcohol. 'The drunken consciousness', said the American psychologist William James (d. 1910), 'is a bit of the mystic consciousness'. It can also be revived by certain mind-expanding drugs. LSD, for instance, has sent subjects back to their earliest childhood and further back to the womb, and, it has been claimed, even to past historical epochs.

In psychotherapy, memories can frequently be recovered by specialized techniques such as psychoanalysis and free-association, which allows material from the unconscious to come to the surface. Hypnosis, as we have seen, is used in order to take people back to earlier periods in their lives and recall long forgotten incidents.

ESB or electrical stimulation of the brain can likewise precipitate recall. Dr Wilder Penfield, formerly director of the Montreal Neurological Institute of McGill University, stated that the brain's playback mechanism can be activated to dredge up the most deeply submerged memories. He found that when he applied electrodes to various points on the surface of the cortex, patients would re-live forgotten episodes of their past.

We are still not aware of the full extent of information accumulated by our minds, nor of the tenacity with which we retain memories of it. George S. Patton (d. 1945), US general of World War II, who was convinced that he had been a 'fighting man' for centuries, could describe battles and sieges of old with startling exactness. He saw himself in the Lydian army meeting Cyrus the Great of Persia (546 B.C.); during the Carthaginian landing at Agrigentum in Sicily (405 B.C.); with Alexander the Great at the walls of Tyre (332 B.C.); on the field of Crécy (1346) during the Hundred Years War; as an officer with Joachim Murat (d. 1815), one of Napoleon's generals. But before we assume reincarnation it should be stated that Patton had been fascinated with military history from his youth. He was keenly interested in past campaigns, had collected an outstanding library of military books, and was intimately familiar with most of their contents.

### Paramnesia and Cryptomnesia

Besides the genuine recall of learning and experience, the mind is capable of some unusual freaks of mis-recall, when a thing experienced becomes distorted, falsified, or fails to be recognized. Such memory anomalies may account for certain seemingly paranormal phenomena.

Thus there is what is called paramnesia, or false memory, the illusion of recognizing something that has never actually been part of one's previous experience. The subject is not aware that he is fantasizing and there is no suggestion of deceit on his part. According to the experts the vast majority of reincarnation reports can be placed in this category. A form of induced paramnesia, it is thought, could help in the selection of the Dalai Lama (see page 30). Having already decided on the most suitable candidate the lama elders could then, either by suggestion or covert guidance, help the boy to 'recognize' his former possessions.

Psychologists also speak of cryptomnesia or hidden memory, that is, the recall of something actually seen or heard before, without the subject consciously recognizing it or remembering the source of the original experience.

In his *Biographia Literaria*, S.T. Coleridge (d. 1834) tells of an illiterate 24-year-old servant girl who in a state of fever spoke in Latin, Greek and Hebrew, 'in very pompous tones and with most distinct enunciation'. On investigation it was found that as a child she had lived in the house of a Protestant pastor who used to recite in a loud voice passages from his favourite books in these languages, and these she must have unconsciously registered in her mind.

Similarly, a teenage Swiss girl of limited education, and below average in intelligence, spoke while in trance with impassioned and glowing rhetoric, using high quality literary German with ease and assurance. Carl Gustav Jung (d. 1961) who studied her case attributed this to the fact that she was dipping into the storehouse of childhood memories of life with her deceased clergyman grandfather.

Cryptomnesia probably also occurs in déjàism where, for instance, a person might see a landscape in childhood, perhaps only in a book illustration or film, and then forget all about it. Years later he sees it in reality, does not remember the earlier experience, and either treats it as a fresh experience in the present life, or attributes it to some paranormal source, possibly even imagining it to be an experience of a past incarnation.

Another well-documented curiosity of recall is xenoglossis, which we have already considered (see page 89), where a person suddenly starts speaking in a language he has never learnt, or in a totally unknown tongue.

All such cases of super-remembering and distorted remembering have been accounted for in various ways. Reincarnationists and spiritualists have their own explanations. Orthodox psychologists speak of them as variations of recall or garbled recall of one's own acquired knowledge. At the same time some psychologists have put forward theories that go beyond the individual's personal store of knowledge, to a store of memories accumulated along the ancestral line.

Now, while biologists have made great progress in establishing the transmission of physical characteristics, the full extent of the part played by heredity in the transmission of mental characteristics is still far from clear. In animals, instinct perhaps codifies the 'mental' past, representing the hereditary inborn experiences of the life lived by the species and transmitted through their genetic structure. The spider's web, the bee's hive, the beaver's dam, are all built out of some obscure inherited pattern that abides in the animals cells.

It has been estimated that in the course of a life span of seventy years, a man receives during his waking moments alone, about 50 trillion bits of information. That is, quite apart from what comes to him in his unconscious states. Every single item of information thus received is registered and permanently stored in its entirety in his mind. In other words, no item of knowledge he has acquired is ever lost. Nothing that a person has seen, heard, read or otherwise experienced, consciously or unconsciously, is obliterated from his mind. Dr Wilder Penfield, mentioned above, stated that the brain holds in its store every single experience of our lives, which it preserves in astonishing detail.

Penfield speaks of a 'ganglionic record' in the brain where this memory is stocked. Other psychologists speak of the neurogram or memory record in the neurones or nerve cells. Still others speak of the experience imprint as an engram or memory trace engraved on the cerebral tissue. But in the view of certain authorities, mind and memory can be regarded in ultimate terms as being independent of matter. The physical brain record might vanish, but the mind record endures permanently, surviving the dissolution of the body.

The crucial question in the matter of inheritance is: do we inherit and retain vestiges of our ancestral past in the form of thoughts, emotions and memories? Our minds have not come to us 'out of the blue', but from a very real past, built up and added to over countless millennia. C.G. Jung said, 'the body has an anatomical prehistory of millions of years, so also the psychic system'.

It has been suggested that just as the biophysical traits are carried by the genes, there may be an inherited mind-and-memory factor, the psychogene, carrying a mental legacy from one generation to the next. This legacy may be transmitted partly through the brain cells which we inherit with the material body, and partly through the hypothetical psychogenes that we inherit with the immaterial psyche.

Some psychologists are of the view that a series of such psychogenes passed on over the centuries, forge a kind of continuing memory chain, a mental continuum built up into instincts, racial and tribal memories, and all the mind-stuff of the antecedent line. It is obvious that there can be no possible break in the chain of succession that leads back to our remotest progenitors and even to our animal past, so that we might at times be motivated by the same impulses that actuated them.

This fascinating study, the 'archaeology' of the mind, is still in its infancy. In one theory our psychic roots go back to a time before the soul was ever embodied. Plato said that the knowledge that all men possess of the eternal verities of truth, beauty, goodness, justice, harmony, proportion, comes from a pre-existent life in a 'spiritual' world of archetypal Ideas or Forms, and that there is no learning or teaching of these great principles, only *anamnesia* or 'recollection' of this earlier knowledge.

Even without invoking the Platonic concept, psychologists state that the mind of the new-born infant is not a *tabula rasa* or clean slate, as one would suppose, but more like a palimpsest, an ancient parchment written upon, then lightly erased, and written upon again, and so on with writing superimposed upon writing through the ages.

The human brain, we are told, has an animal ancestry. But starting from the human species alone, a man's brain registers experiences even before he is born. It is known that the brain of the foetus is an active and inquisitive agent, ceaselessly absorbing impressions of what happens while it is within the womb (Walker, 1977, p.103). This forms part of the individual's personal memory, and to this store he will continue to add during his childhood and throughout his later lifetime.

Sigmund Freud (d. 1939) suggested that prenatal memories may be responsible for certain feelings of déjà vu, and when, for instance, a person dreams of a place that seems familiar and gives him the feeling of having been there before, 'we may interpret the place as being his mother's genitals or her body'. A less exceptionable theory has it that the experiences of the foetus, which include the mother's emotional reactions, transmitted to the sensitive organism she bears in her womb, may account for many of the déjàist intimations and 'memories' that occur to the individual in later life.

The mind therefore teems not only with the individual's personal experiences, foetal, childhood and adult, but also with the parental, and possibly ancestral, racial and animal memories which he inherits. This mighty taproot of the past, with all its subsidiary adventitious rootlets, nourishes the psyche we now possess. Nothing ever perishes entirely, and some chance stimulus may cause an incident or scene to spring to consciousness from deep within us, and give us a glimpse of some experience we ourselves did not personally encounter.

Virginia Tighe of Bridey Murphy fame did not believe in reincarnation herself, and attributed her remembrance of her past life under hypnosis to genetic memory. Said Virginia, 'Just as the salmon remembers the river its ancestors swam up to spawn, or fledgling swallows the flight south, so I may have remembered'.

In 1930 Marie Skotniki, a 4-year old girl of Warsaw, who spoke only Polish, started talking to herself in a language that no one about her could understand. It was eventually identified as pure Gaelic. Interestingly enough, and whatever we may make of it, her grandfather came from the Scottish Hebrides. In 1965 a three-year-old Israeli boy began to speak fluently in Biblical Hebrew, played the harp as King David had done, and exhorted his people to follow him into battle.

Such instances as this lend support to the theory that what is sometimes taken to be a remembrance of a past incarnation may in fact be the experience of a progenitor in the subject's hereditary line. For some as yet unexplained reason, a person picks up odds and ends of what his ancestors knew, sometimes vividly enough to recall fragments of speech, names, places and other details.

**The Collective Unconscious**

Yet the sources of our knowledge are not restricted to our ancestral line. Besides the remembrance we might have from the direct line of our ancestors, there is a still larger pool of memory into which we all dip from time to time. This is the collective unconscious, the entire memory bank, not only of the individual, the family, the tribe, but of the whole human race. The Islamic philosopher Averroes (d. 1198) taught that while we have separate bodies we do not have separate minds, and are 'like an aquatic plant with many heads showing above water, but all meeting in one great root beneath the surface'.

The collective unconscious represents the sum total of all the psychogenetic material or thought-substance of humanity. C.G. Jung who first put forward the theory of the collective unconscious spoke of it as a transpersonal, universal, archaic nucleus of memories shared by all the members of the human race. Some part of the mind in all individuals is the common property of all. According to this theory, all minds are connected at one level to a higher consciousness, so that the whole of mankind is united in a vast empire of mind, built out of the personal exploration of all individuals past and present.

In theory therefore we are capable of having access to all minds, contemporary and historical. Each one of us is a citizen of the limitless territory of the cosmic mind of which we are part and with which we are sometimes in communication. Moss and Keeton refer to the theory 'that experiences and actions of all time are stored away in some incredible psychic computer' from which, with the right programming, knowledge of the past can be drawn (1979, p.16).

Although memory is naturally associated with living and animate beings, the possibility of a kind of memory-aura inhering in inanimate matter has also been suggested. Here again we are confronted with the hypothesis of a mind that is everywhere present and of memories that are virtually never lost. They are recorded in the minds of men and in the register of the collective unconscious, and in the countless imprints of all that is done, felt and thought, that are left on the things around us.

We are indeed the 'heirs of all the ages'.

Sensitives are able to pick up the thoughts and emotions associated with objects. Thus, by holding a ring or any small personal belonging, they can give information about its owner or owners, and of the major incidents connected with them. In psychical research such an article is known as a 'psychometric object', which is anything that can trigger recall of something associated with it. There may even be psychometric individuals or psychometric places, serving as links with the past, and inciting psychic activity and receptivity in those who find themselves in their vicinity.

In his *Memories, Dreams, Reflections*, C.G. Jung relates an experience that would seem to confirm this. In 1924 he used to be persistently awakened at night by a distinct feeling that a number of young people were playing music and singing just outside his house. But when he opened the window to investigate there was no one there and everything was still. His enquiries some time later revealed that in medieval times it was customary for the young men of the town when about to leave for the wars to meet near the place where his house was situated, and hold a farewell celebration. Jung was aparently able to tap the memory of an event that lay dormant in the locality itself.

Theosophists speak of the akashik records, a term derived from the Sanskrit word *akasha*, meaning 'ether', which constitute a kind of cosmic library in which is permanently stored everything that has ever been thought, felt, said or done from the beginning of time. These archives figuratively represent a kind of universal memory-plane, a mind repository, not far out in the empyrean, but permeating everything around us, so that we can in truth 'find tongues in trees, books in the running brooks, and sermons in stones'. We are constantly scanning lines from these primeval scripts, of which we are vouchsafed an occasional glimpse in flickering fashion.

A more extended interpretation of what is known as extra-sensory perception, could reveal the miracle of the interaction of mind with mind that does not need the hypothesis of occultism, spiritualism or reincarnation. We can receive thoughts and information, sometimes by an effort of will, sometimes spontaneously, and sometimes by chance, for which no materialistic explanation can provide a satisfactory answer. We can preserve and transmit knowledge and impresions by means other than the known sensory channels, and this process is not modified by distance or time.

All of us, although we are not consciously aware of it, are 'carriers' of ancient stores of information, and our mere presence in the vicinity of another person, not necessarily psychic, can in certain situations enable him to pick up some of that material from our minds. Indeed even the presence of that other person is not an essential prerequisite for the transmission and reception of that information.

It has been said that there are no such things as lost books and closed minds. Some item of knowledge, once known to a person long dead, a medieval monk for instance, and now forgotten for centuries, might be unconsciously transmitted from mind to mind by individuals in successive generations, and then suddenly come to light by being telepathically picked up and brought to consciousness by someone now living.

Every human being is a link with the past and carries records of experiences he knows nothing about. He taps the minds of others and his own mind is likewise tapped. Psychologists speak of the possibility of such paranormal acquisition of knowledge by mind-tapping on a virtually limitless scale.

We do not know the precise mechanism of this mind-tapping, which is an unconscious process and not available to order, but it is constantly going on. We are part of a vast network of interrelated minds, and the full potential of an individual mind is much greater than we can conceive.

The medieval scholastics saw man as *capax universi*, capable of bringing the whole universe within the range of his experience.

# 7
# Karmic Justice and Divine Mercy

Critics of reincarnation frequently oppose the doctrine on moral and religious grounds. Reincarnation, they argue, has seldom been a motive force in anyone's life. On the contrary, it has a stultifying effect on moral effort and spiritual development.

The belief is seldom held with any intensity of conviction. How many people, east or west, are prompted to do good because they feel they are weaving their future destiny thread by thread, and will return to earth in a better situation as a result? Those who bear their present suffering with resignation do so because they often have no other choice. They ascribe it to their 'kismet' (fate), to the will of God, or to sheer bad luck, and not to their karma resulting from some undisclosed shortcomings of a former life.

In spite of what is claimed for it on moral grounds, reincarnation has no great moral significance and is ethically unacceptable. It renders one callous to the sufferings of others. If poverty, ill-health and pain, are the consequences of a wicked life in a previous incarnation, then any attempt to relieve them is tantamount to interference with the decrees of providence. And if we treat someone with cruelty, who must therefore have been cruel in a past life, we are to be regarded as the instruments of divine retribution and are ourselves blameless. Otherwise, who will punish the sinner? And where does the process end? Those who suffer obviously merit suffering.

In India, the rigid observance of the caste system, based on birth, might be regarded as the practical outcome of belief in karma and its consequences. A man who is born into a brahmin family has earned his superior status. Conversely, people who are lower in the social scale deserve to be there. If the gods have placed a man in a situation of inferiority, it hardly behoves others to try to change the order of things. For this reason some people dismiss reincarnation as 'old brahmin moonshine', as Sir Walter Scott (d. 1832) dubbed it in one of his novels.

The great, the famous, the better off, who so grandiloquently endorse the doctrine, may find that it gives them a sense of personal satisfaction. It establishes their own past advancement, and in a way ensures, in their own minds at least, their better status in the next life.

The argument is developed in other ways. If a man has bestowed upon him the blessings of an abundant life and the gift of this world's largess, it is because he has earned it by useful work in a previous incarnation. There is no reason why he should make any attempt in the present life to resist the lures of enjoyment and pleasure, and not make the best of what are literally heaven-sent gifts. If his actions turn out to be harmful, well then, there is always another chance, and all the time in the world to make amends.

Further, if people are reborn according to their deserts, then the successful, the affluent, the powerful, should be morally better than the less fortunate, because they are reaping the benefits of a past life of virtue, and they should, like precocious children and their talents, pick up their virtues where they left off. The virtues of an earlier incarnation must to some extent be reflected in this life as well. But more often than not we find that the richer and more successful are morally no better, and sometimes considerably worse, than their poorer brethren.

Finally, if spiritual evolution is the chief index of our advancement, then as a result of mankind's accumulating experiences, extending over thousands of years, we might expect the whole human race to be showing signs of greater spirituality than before. But again, we do not find this to the the case. Judging by the present state of the world, mankind cannot be said to be improving spiritually. There is no upward movement, but rather a decline, reflected in a growing emphasis on material values.

Even Hinduism, a bastion of reincarnation, predicts the progressive decline in the moral and spiritual climate of the world, from the past golden age to the present Kali Yuga or Black

Era in which we now live. The Iron Curtain countries, till recently religious, and China formerly the largest Buddhist nation in the world, are now atheistic. The greater part of the western hemisphere, once proudly forming 'Christendom', today pays little heed to things of the spirit.

Another side of the moral problem concerns memory. Despite the reasons put forward by reincarnationists to explain why people do not remember their past lives, the memory argument still stands. If we are to learn from our past mistakes and benefit from the lessons that our previous incarnations have to teach us, it would only be reasonable to expect that we should remember our past, so that we might know wherein we had failed. It seems unfair that we should have to suffer for some action of which we are given no conscious reminder.

The argument advanced that we have forgotten our past lives, for whatever reason, would seem to cast doubt on the theory itself. Perhaps we do not remember our so-called past incarnations, because we never had them in the first place. The fact that we live out our lives with no continuing memory of the past would suggest that we are separate, new and unique selves, and not a continuing chain of different personalities bound together by a common soul, as is claimed.

The English philosopher John Locke (d. 1704) imagined an individual now living, who has the immortal soul or spirit that once inhabited the body of Nestor the ancient Greek hero during the siege of Troy. Can he be concerned with Nestor's actions, or think of those actions as his own? Without Nestor's consciousness he cannot be the same person. The German mathematician and thinker Gottfried Wilhelm Leibniz (d. 1716) makes the same point. He asks, 'What good would it do to become ruler of China if you forget what you have been. Would it not be the same if God had destroyed you and created a ruler of China?'

Above all, reincarnation has been claimed as a supremely just doctrine, providing all souls with the opportunity to evolve. The more rigorous opponents, however, condemn it as a philosophical absurdity, crudely animistic and spiritually untenable. The truth of its ultimate justice, in their view, could only be established if all souls had started their evolution together at the same time, and were equally equipped to face the trials and temptations of the world, which trials and temptations would themselves have to be the same for each person.

It is clear that all souls could not have begun their incarnations at the same time, for then the population of the world would have been more or less stable. We know that the earth's population has been increasing at an ever accelerating pace. It was 250 million in A.D. 1, and is now over 4,000 million. If new souls are being put into circulation all the time, they could obviously not be facing the same situation as those souls which embarked on their careers earlier.

To uphold the claim of strict justice, in the beginning all souls would have had to be either perfect, or all equally imperfect. If all souls were perfect to begin with, what was the need for them to be incarnated at all? If they were all imperfect, did they share identical weaknesses? Were they endowed with the same strengths? Did they have to face the same situations? If not, then souls must have been sent into the world with varying attributes, some weak and some strong, and would have had to contend against varying odds. It would appear, then, that the responsibility for any failure as a result of these inequalities should rightly lie not with the souls concerned, but with God.

For this reason, it has been argued, reincarnation theorists who affirm that human lives are endlessly put on trial again and again, merely postpone to infinity the problems of inequality and injustice that they refuse to face and cannot solve.

**Karma**

Underlying the philosophy on which the whole edifice of reincarnation has been raised is, as we have seen, the idea of karma, the fixed and unalterable law of cause and consequence in human affairs, by which a person's present life is determined by his actions in a past life, and his future life will be determined by his present actions.

Karma is one of three basic forms of determinism. The first is causality, which is the scientific face of determinism, explaining the principles of physical cause and effect: tuberculosis results from infection with the tubercule bacillus. The second is kismet or fate, which is the religious face of determinism: a man contracts tuberculosis because such is the inscrutable will of divine providence. The third is karma, the reincarnationist face of determinism, explaining human affairs in terms of human action past and present: a man contracts tuberculosis because, for example, he impaled prisoners in a previous life.

Karma is thus seen as a law of relentless and inescapable retribution, determined by strict and undeviating measure, and dealt out with unmitigated justice. Nothing is exempt from the operation of this law, by which each casual deed and idle word, and in fact each thought which flits through the mind, is placed without exception in the scales by which we are judged.

In popular usage the terms destiny, fate, kismet, presuppose the existence of a more powerful law that imposes a limitation on the free will of the individual. Man can exercise no control over this higher law, and would be wise to accept it. The Chinese philosopher Confucius wrote, 'If a man succeeds it is well. If he fails it is also well. He must recognize the operation of *ming* (destiny)'. Marcus Aurelius, Roman Emperor and Stoic philosopher, said that the mark of a wise man is that he welcomes what befalls him and what is being spun for him by the Fates.

Both free will and chance are illusions. What looks like chance arises from the profoundest sources of destiny. Our health and sickness, our happiness and misery, are not due to heredity, environment, planetary influences or luck, but to law and destiny, and these are determined not by chance but necessity. A man, in effect, cannot will and decide otherwise than he does.

'Chance is a word devoid of meaning', said Voltaire. The Belgian writer Maurice Maeterlinck wrote, 'The man for whom the hour of misfortune has sounded is the subject of preceding forces that combine to bring him to the exact moment and place where tears lie in wait for him.'

To many people karma is a forbidding doctrine. There is something cold and calculating about the exactness with which justice is meted out. It seems impossible to escape from the clutches of this iron law. Man is chained by the decree of necessity to the great wheel of fate which turns remorselessly and without cessation. Nothing it seems can break the shackles that bind him to this wheel.

Even in our imperfect society advanced legislation makes certain concessions to those who have violated the social law. So, it is argued, if human society takes human weaknesses into account, surely a heavenly dispensation has an understanding of human shortcomings as well. Most religions recognize the value of self-denial, penance, prayer, religious observance, charity and good works, as a means of expiating the adverse effects of wrong doing.

The most important and effective of all these measures is said to be faith in the grace of God. All the major religions emphasize the redeeming virtues of faith. This concept, known to the Hindus as *bhakti*, meaning God's grace or compassion, was introduced into popular Hinduism through Christian sources in about A.D.300. Sincere faith following sincere repentance wipes out the effects of sin, frees man from the burden of karma and from the bondage of eternal rebirth.

God's grace overrides karmic destiny. Karma is founded on law, *bhakti* is founded on love. Karma is divine justice, *bhakti* is divine mercy. And for men of faith God's mercy is greater than God's justice.

In the strict reincarnationist view, say the critics, *bhakti* is never invoked, because if it were it would put an end to the theory of reincarnation. God therefore does not actively enter into the reincarnationist scheme of things. Everything is mechanistic and predetermined, hardly necessitating belief in a divine providence. In a manner of speaking the teaching is both atheistic and materialistic. It does not need God since the machinery of destiny works on its own with mathematical precision. It is materialistic because the arena of the soul's operation and the theatre of its redemption is the earth and nothing but the earth.

According to the exponents of reincarnation, only those who attain the highest state of moral and spiritual perfection are exempt from returning again to the material world in which lesser mortals are condemned to pass their days. The majority of mankind, being by nature weak and far from saintly, has little hope of ever breaking free from the relentless cycle of birth-death-rebirth.

The theosophists say that the purpose of successive rebirths is man's eventual all-round perfection. Not only spiritual but intellectual and physical perfection as well, and this needs schooling and experience in a material environment (Hodson, 1967, p.49). In terms of fallible humanity it means that every mortal soul faces the prospect of recurrent dawns and endless sunsets without purpose. The ordinary man is launched on a journey of which his life's course from the cradle to the coffin is but a single stage, with birth as the beginning of the day's trek, and death the night's halt, and this pilgrimage is without end, with birth and death succeeding birth and death aeon after aeon through all eternity. Even modern authorities speak of subjects reincarnating from the days of Atlantis and Lemuria, and sometimes earlier.

The answer to the question posed by the Roman philosopher Seneca, 'How long this self-same round?' would appear to be, 'For ever and ever'. The Neoplatonists believed that only the highest type of human being ever attained perfection, and that the vast majority of men and women were never released from the cycle of rebirth. Man lives through what has been called 'perpetual metamorphoses', ever assuming a new personality, ever putting on a new mask, and returning *ad infinitum* to play his empty part in the charade of human existence.

**Eternal Return**

In ancient philosophy the return of the soul to its earthly habitation in life after life was seen as part of a much larger cycle of cosmic periodicities. We proceed through causality, determinism, and the endless sequence of birth-death-rebirth, to the final conclusion of eternal recurrence. The Greeks referred to this unending movement of all things in unbroken succession as *anakuklosis*, 'encycling', suggesting that all things are bound to a wheel and will in time return to their original positions. The world is not static and nothing simply is, everything is becoming. And this process is circular.

The ancient astronomers believed that the constellations, stars and planets in the course of their movement through the heavens returned after a long period of time to the exact places they once occupied, and when this occurred everything that had taken place at the time of their earlier disposition would start all over again in the same order. History would repeat itself in every detail.

The course of encycling involves the world in periodical destruction by fire (Gk. *ekpyrosis*), flood (*kataklysmos*), and storm (*lailaposis*), followed by regeneration (*metakosmesis*) in never ceasing periodicities. The word for the rebirth of the planetary, constellatory or cosmic systems after their periodical destruction was *palingenesis* (Gk. 'again-born'), a term later used by the rosicrucians for the process of restoring a substance from its ashes, a secret they claimed to have achieved with, among other things, the rose, which they burnt in a crucible and then restored. The reincarnationists adopted the term palingenesis as a synonym for reincarnation, or the rebirth of the soul in another body after the death of its former corporeal habitation.

Belief in the periodic destruction of the universe and its restoration to its original state is based on the doctrine of eternal recurrence. According to this doctrine, all events in the history of the world are an exact reproduction of events that preceded them in the earlier cycle. The future will repeat the present, as the present repeats the past.

The philosopher Pythagoras, greatest of the Greek advocates of reincarnation, said that the movement of time was not linear, that is, in a straight line, but cyclic, and that all things recur again and again and are endlessly repeated.

Eudemus, a follower of Aristotle, told his pupils, 'If we may believe the Pythagoreans, I shall once more gossip with you with this little staff in my hand, and again as now you will be sitting before me, and so will it be with all the rest.'

The Stoics made this notion popular in Rome, that all things in the end come back to exactly where they were before; that the movement of history is an unending process of expansion and decline, with all things being repeated each time in the same sequence and in exact detail as they were.

Sir Thomas Browne (d. 1682) refers to the ancient belief that 'Men are lived over again, and the world is now as it was in ages past.'

The German poet and philosopher Johann Wolfgang von Goethe (d. 1832) wrote, 'I am certain that I have been here, as I am now, a thousand times before, and I hope to return a thousand times.'

The same fundamental theme is presented in Friedrich Nietzsche's *Thus Spake Zarathustra* (1884). 'Everything goes, everything returns, everything dies and blossoms once more. Everything breaks and is integrated anew. Everything eternally builds again the identical house of existence'.

Peter Ouspensky, Russian mystic and pupil of Gurdjieff went

so far as to say that everyone would be born again, on the same day, in the same house, of the same parents, would meet the same people, love and marry the same persons, and act out life exactly as before.

Many people would find the idea of eternal recurrence an essentially restrictive concept, binding man eternally to the temporal cosmos and to cyclic time. To return to earth would be bad enough for some, but to return to the identical situation seems utterly without meaning, and to those who have suffered, horrifying in the extreme. It is futile and non-progressive, involving no true development or spiritual advancement.

Because of the awesome inevitability of rebirth without apparent end, reincarnation has been called 'the nightmare of eastern philosophy'. Far from regarding it as a sublime prospect, opening up a future of many beautiful dawns, the great religions of the east that subscribe to the doctrine, 'view the prospect with much anxiety', says Professor J. Paul Williams of Mount Holyoke College, Massachusetts, and the one major function of these religions is to teach men how to avoid being reborn (Head and Cranston, 1961, p.281), and so escape from the prison-house of karma. For them the heartfelt plea is, 'Stop the Wheel, I want to get off!'

Yet according to the law of karma nothing in our power can possibly arrest the motion of the wheel, and we can never escape the predicament of our existence, unless we become perfect in an almost divine sense.

Whether the matter is considered in cosmic terms, as in eternal recurrence, or in human terms, as in reincarnation, the idea of monotonous repetition seems to be without purpose. The return of the soul to body after body to attain perfection makes it a virtually unattainable and infinite task, and so a futile one.

**Other Worlds**

On the other hand, the eternal existence of the soul, it has been argued, need not necessarily mean its eternal sojourn on the material plane to exhaust all the experiences of earthly existence. There are other possible futures besides reincarnation in which the soul might evolve. In an infinite universe there must be infinite possibilities for growth and development and more significant levels than a material environment can provide.

The Moslem Sufi theologian Muhammad al-Ghazali (d. 1111) wrote, 'This world is but one stage of eternity. It is a market opened in a wilderness where those who are travelling on their way to God may prepare provisions for their journey.' The Russian Buriat mystic, George Gurdjieff said that the human soul after repeated trials in different worlds becomes a pure spirit. Edgar Cayce, reincarnationist though he was, spoke of other realms of development.

The grave is not a blind alley leading nowhere, as the materialists tell us. Neither is it a circular highway, as is implied in reincarnation, leading the weary wayfarer repeatedly back to the same place, like a man lost in the desert. There exists a different reality and an active afterlife, from the standpoint of which our life on earth will appear like a mirage.

Towards the end of his life, Albert Einstein said, 'Here on earth I have done my job.' Death is final in the material sphere. It is a gateway opening into another broader thoroughfare, with vistas of new and varied experiences. Benjamin Franklin expressed the hope that on his death, when his body like an old book became food for worms, the work might reappear in a new edition, 'revised and corrected by the Author'. In the metaphor of Oliver Wendell Holmes, the soul leaves its low-valuted past for a vaster more noble dome, and knows its former haunts no more. Or, as Thomas Carlyle put it, 'Death and birth are the vesper and matin bells that summon mankind to sleep and to rise refreshed for new advancement.'

Most religious traditions give support to the idea that there are many spheres in the hereafter, metaphorically spoken of as heaven, hell, purgatory, and so on. Some are designed for purification, others provide further trials and tests, all offer scope for advancement.

Jesus spoke of the 'many mansions' of the other world (John 14.2). Christians point out that in Greek the word *monē*, which is translated 'mansion', also means stage or station. After death life continues, but in other worlds beyond our present habitation. Such was the opinion of Irenaeus and other early Church Fathers.

In this alternative view of life beyond death, the next world extends outwards on all sides in ascending and descending degrees. The sequel to our life here is a graded series of stages allowing for the soul's progress.

According to its capacity the soul passes from sphere to sphere with increased understanding, growing richer in experience as it moves upward, until it reaches the final sphere of the highest heaven and the glory of the Divine Light.

# Bibliography


Abd ar-Rahim ibn Ahmad al-Qadi (ed). *Islamic Book of the Dead*, Diwan Press, London, 1977

Abhedananda, Swami. *Reincarnation*, 1899; 10th ed., Ramakrishna Vedanta Math, Calcutta, 1973

Addison, J.T. *Life Beyond Death in the Beliefs of Mankind*, Allen & Unwin, London, 1958

Alexander, Robert. *A Psychical Experience*, Regency Press, London, 1970

Alger, William R. *A Critical History of the Doctrine of a Future Life*, 10th ed., Widdleton, New York, 1880

Allport, G. *Personality: A Psychological Interpretation*, Holt, New York, 1937

Andreas, P., and Adams, G. *Between Heaven and Earth*, Harrap, London, 1967

Aurobindo, Sri. *The Problem of Rebirth*, Sri Aurobindo Ashram, Pondicherry, 1972

Austin, Mary. *Experiences Facing Death*, Bobbs-Merrill, New York, 1931

Baillie, John. *And the Life Everlasting*, Scribner, New York, 1933; Oxford University Press, 1934

Barlow, Fred. *Mental Prodigies*, Hutchinson, London, 1951

Barratt, William. *Deathbed Visions*, Methuen, London, 1926

Battersby, H.P. *Man Outside Himself*, Rider, London, n.d.

Bernstein, Morey. *The Search for Bridey Murphy*, Doubleday, New York; Hutchinson, London, 1956

Bertholet, Alfred. *Transmigration of Souls*, Harpers, New York, 1909

Besant, Annie. *Karma*, Theosophical Publishing House, London, 1890

Besant, Annie. *Death – And After?* Theosophical Publishing House, London; The Path, New York, 1893

Besant, Annie. *Reincarnation*, 8th ed., Theosophical Publishing House, Adyar; Wheaton, Illinois, 1963

Birrell, F.F.L. and Lucas, F.L. *The Art of Dying: An Anthology*, Hogarth Press, London, 1930

Bloxham, Dulcie. *Who Was Ann Ockenden?*, Neville Spearman, London, 1958

Boros, Ladislaus. *The Moment of Truth: Mysterium Mortis*, Burns & Oates, London, 1965. Published as *The Mystery of Death*, Seabury Press, New York, 1965

Bose, S.C. *A Case of Reincarnation* (Shanti Devi), Satsang, Calcutta, 1952

Bozzano, E. *Discarnate Influence on Human Life*, Watkins, London, 1938

Bradley, Dennis. *Towards the Stars*, Spiritualist Association, London, 1924

Brandon, S.G.F. *History, Time and Destiny*, Manchester University Press, 1965

Brandon, S.G.F. *The Judgment of the Dead*, Weidenfield & Nicolson, London, 1967; Scribner, New York, 1969

Brewster, David. *More Worlds Than One*, 2nd ed., Morton, London, 1901

Bucke, Richard M. *Cosmic Consciousness*, Innes, Philadelphia, 1905; Olympia Press, London, 1972

Budge, E.A. Wallis (ed.). *The Book of the Dead*, 2nd ed., Routledge, London; Dover, New York, 1967

Bultmann, Rudolf. *History and Eschatology: the Presence of Eternity*, Harper, New York, 1962

Cannon, Sir Alexander. *The Shadow of Destiny: the Power of Karma*, Aquarian Press, London, 1970

Carty, Charles M. *Two Stigmatists: Padre Pio and Teresa Neumann*, Veritas, Dublin, 1956

Cayce, Edgar Evans. *Edgar Cayce on Atlantis*, Paperback Library, New York, 1968

Cerminara, Gina. *Many Mansions*, William Sloan, New York, 1950; Spearman, London, 1967

Cerminara, Gina. *The World Within*, William Sloan, New York, 1957; C.W. Daniel, London, 1973

Cerminara, Gina. *Many Lives, Many Loves*, Morrow, New York, 1963

Chadwick, N.K. *The Druids*, University Press, Cardiff, 1966

Challoner, H.K. *The Wheel of Rebirth*, Theosophical Publishing House, London, 1969

Charles, R.H. *Eschatology*, 2nd ed., Bailey, London; Schocken, New York, 1963

Choron, Jacques. *Death and Western Thought*, Collier-Macmillan, London and New York, 1963

Cockayne, E.A. *Inherited Abnormalities of the Skin*, Oxford University Press, 1933

Cornillier, P.E. *The Survival of the Soul*, Kegan Paul, Trench, Trubner, London, 1921

Cullmann, Oscar. *Immortality of the Soul or Resurrection of the Dead?* Epworth Press, London, 1958

Cummins, Geraldine. *The Road to Immortality*, Nicholson & Watson, London, 1935

Cummins, Geraldine. *Mind in Life and Death*, Aquarian Press, London, 1956

Dahl, M.E. *The Resurrection of the Body*, SCM Press, London, 1962

D'Assier, Adolph. *Posthumous Humanity*, translated and annotated by H.S. Olcott, Redway, London, 1887

David, N.E. *Karma and Reincarnation in Israelitism*, Mellor, London, 1908

Davids, C.A.F. Rhys. *Indian Religion and Survival*, Allen & Unwin, London, 1934

Delanne, G. *Documents pour servir à l'étude de la réincarnation*, Editions de la B.P.S., Paris, 1924

De Silva, Lynn A. *Reincarnation in Christian and Buddhist Thought*, Christian Literature Society of Ceylon, Colombo, 1968

De Vesme, Caesar. *Peoples of Antiquity*, Rider, London, 1931

Devlin, Barbara Lynne. *I am Mary Shelley*, Condor, New York, 1977

Ducasse, C.J. *A Critical Examination of the Belief in a Life After Death*, C.C. Thomas, Springfield, Illinois, 1961

Ebon, Martin. *Reincarnation in the Twentieth Century*, New American Library, New York, 1969; Signet Books, London, 1970

Eccles, J.C. (ed.). *The Brain and Conscious Experience*, Springer, Heidelberg, 1966

Ecstein, Gustav. *The Body Has a Head*, Collins, London, 1971

Eddy, Sherwood. *You Will Survive After Death*, Rinehart, New York, 1950

Eisler, Robert. *Orpheus the Fisher*, Watkins, London, 1921

Eliade, Mircea. *The Myth of Eternal Return*, Routledge, London, 1954

Elliot, Gil. *Twentieth-Century Book of the Dead*, Scribner, New York, 1972; Penguin, Harmondsworth, 1973

Evans-Wentz, W.Y. *The Doctrine of Re-Birth*, Mahabodhi Press, Colombo, 1921

Evans-Wentz, W.Y. *The Tibetan Book of the Dead*, 3rd ed., Oxford University Press, 1957

Feifel, Herman (ed.). *The Meaning of Death*, McGraw-Hill, New York, 1959

Fiore, Edith. *You Have Been Here Before*, Sphere Books, London, 1980.

Flournoy, Theodore. *From India to the Planet Mars*, 1900. University Books, New York, 1963

Fodor, Nandor. *Encyclopedia of Psychic Science*, Arthurs Press, London, 1934

Fodor, Nandor. *Between Two Worlds*, Prentice-Hall, New York, 1964

Ford, Arthur. *The Life Beyond Death*, Putnam, New York, 1971; Sphere Books, London, 1974

Freud, Sigmund. *The Psychopathology of Everyday Life*, Hogarth Press, London, 1960

Fulton, Robert (ed.). *Death and Identity*, Wiley, New York, 1965

Furst, Jeffrey. *Edgar Cayce's Story of Jesus*, Coward, McCann, Geoghegan, New York, 1960

Frazer, J.G. *The Belief in Immortality and the Worship of the Dead*, Macmillan, London, 1929; Barnes & Noble, New York, 1968

Gardner, Martin. *Fads and Fallacies in the Name of Science*, Dover, New York, 2nd ed., 1957

Gerhardie, William. *Resurrection*, Cassell, London, 1934

Glaskin, G.M. *Windows of the Mind: The Christos Experiment*, Wildwood House, London, 1974

Godwin, John. *Occult America*, Doubleday, New York, 1972

Goodman, Jeffrey. *Psychic Archaeology*, Wildwood House, London, 1977

Grant, Joan. *Far Memory*, Harper, New York, 1956; also published as *Time Out of Mind*, Arthur Barker, London, 1956.

Grant, Joan, and Kelsey, Denys. *Many Lifetimes*, Gollancz London; Pocket Books, New York, 1969

Greenhouse, Herbert. *The Book of Psychic Knowledge*, Angus & Robertson, London; Taplinger, New York, 1973

Guirdham, Arthur. *The Cathars and Reincarnation*, Spearman, London, 1970

Guirdham, Arthur. *We Are One Another*, Spearman, London, 1974

Guirdham, Arthur. *The Lake and the Castle*, Spearman, London, 1976

Guirdham, Arthur. *The Psyche in Medicine*, Spearman, London, 1978

Gunaratna, V.F. *Rebirth Explained*, Buddhist Publication Society, Kandy, 1971

Gupta, L.D., *et al. An Inquiry into the Case of Shanti Devi*, International Aryan League, Delhi, 1936

Harlow, S. Ralph. *A Life After Death*, Gollancz, London, 1961

Hart, Hornell. *The Enigma of Survival: The Case For and Against an After Life*, Rider, London, 1959

Hartley, Christine. *A Case for Reincarnation*, Hale, London, 1972

Haynes, E.S.P. *The Belief in Personal Immortality*, Watts, London; Putnam, New York, 1913

Head, Joseph, and Cranston, S.L. (eds.). *Reincarnation: an East-West Anthology*, Julian Press, New York, 1961

Herzog, Edgar. *Psyche and Death*, Hodder & Stoughton, London, 1966

Hick, John. *Death and Eternal Life*, Collins, Fount Paperbacks, London, 1979

Hill, Douglas. *Return from the Dead*, Macdonald, London, 1970

Hill, J. Arthur. *Man is a Spirit*, Cassell, London, 1918

Hives, Frank. *Glimpses into Infinity*, Lane, London, 1931

Hodson, Geoffrey. *Reincarnation, Fact or Fallacy?* 5th ed., Theosophical Publishing House, London and Adyar; Quest Book, Wheaton, Illinois, 1967

Hogg, A.G. *Karma and Redemption*, Christian Literature Society, Madras, 1970

Howe, Quincy. *Reincarnation for the Christian*, Westminster Press, Philadelphia, 1974

Hügel, F. von. *Eternal Life*, T. & T. Clark, Edinburgh, 1912

Hughes, G.E. *On Having the Past All Over Again*, Victoria University College, New Zealand, 1951

Hull, C.L. *Hypnosis and Suggestibility*, Appleton-Century, New York, 1933

Humphreys, Christmas. *Karma and Rebirth*, Wisdom of the East Series, John Murray, London, 1943

Hunt, Douglas. *Exploring the Occult*, Pan Books, London, 1964

Huxley, T.H., and Julian. *Evolution and Ethics, 1893-1943*, Pilot Press, London; Harper, New York, 1947

Iverson, Jeffrey. *More Lives Than One*, Pan Books, London, 1977

James, William. *The Varieties of Religious Experience*, Longmans, Green, London and New York, 1902

Jast, L. Stanley. *Reincarnation and Karma*, Barnes, New York; Bodley Head, London, 1960

Jayatilleke, K.N. *Survival and Karma in Buddhist Perspective*, Buddhist Publication Society, Kandy, 1969

Johansson, Rune. *The Psychology of Nirvana*, Allen & Unwin, London; Anchor Books, New York, 1969

Johnson, Raynor. *The Imprisoned Splendour*, Hodder & Stoughton, London, 1953

Judge, William Q. *The Scope of Reincarnation*, Cunningham Press, Los Angeles, 2nd ed., 1930

Jung, C.G. *Memories, Dreams, Reflections*, Collins and Routledge, London, 1963

Kardec, Allan. *Le Livre des Esprits*, Librairie des Sciences Psychiques, Paris, 1922

Keck, Leander E. *Perspectives on Death*, Abingdon Press, Nashville, Tennessee, 1969

Kline, Milton, V. (ed.). *A Scientific Report on 'The Search for Bridey Murphy'*, Julian Press, New York, 1956

Kübler-Ross, Elizabeth. *On Death and Dying*, Macmillan, New York, 1969; Tavistock Publications, London, 1970

Lamont, Corliss. *The Illusion of Immortality*, 3rd ed., Philosophical Library, New York; Elek, London, 1962

Langley, Noel. *Edgar Cayce on Reincarnation*, Paperback Library, New York, 1967

Lawton, G. *The Drama of Life After Death*, Constable, London, 1933

Leadbeater, C.W. *The Soul's Growth Through Reincarnation*, 3 vols., 2nd ed., Theosophical Publishing House, Madras, 1948-1950

Lehrer, Keither (ed.). *Freedom and Determinism*, Random House, New York, 1966

Leonard, Gladys Osborn. *My Life in Two Worlds*, Cassell, London, 1931

Lester, Reginald M. *In Search of the Hereafter*, Harrap, London, 1952

Lévy-Bruhl, Lucien. *The 'Soul' of the Primitive*, Allen & Unwin, London, 1928

Lewis, H.D. *The Self and Immortality*, Macmillan, London; Seabury Press, New York, 1973

Lodge, Sir Oliver. *The Survival of Man*, Methuen, London, 1919

Lowes, J.L. *The Road to Xanadu: A Study in the Ways of the Imagination*, Constable, London, 1927

Lucas, John. *The Freedom of the Will*, Oxford University Press, 1970

Lutoslawski, Wincenty. *Pre-Existence and Reincarnation*, Allen & Unwin, London, 1928

Lyttleton, Edith. *Our Superconscious Mind*, Philip Allan, London, 1931

Manning, Matthew. *The Strangers*, W.H. Allen, London, 1978

Marchant, James (ed.). *Immortality*, Putnam, New York, 1924

Martin, Eva (ed.). *The Ring of Return*, Philip Alan, London, 1927

Masters, R.E.L., and Houston, Jean. *The Varieties of Psychedelic Experience*, Blond, London, 1967

McGatch, Milton C. *Death: Meaning and Mortality in Christian Thought and Contemporary Culture*, Seabury Press, New York, 1969

Mead, G.R.S. (ed.). *The Divine Pymander of Hermes Trismegistus*, Shrine of Wisdom, London, 1923

Millard, Joseph. *Edgar Cayce: Man of Miracles*, Spearman, London, 1961; Fawcett World Library, New York, 1967

Miller, R. DeWitt. *Reincarnation*, Paperback Library, New York, 1956

Mills, Liston O. (ed.). *Perspectives on Death*, Abingdon Press, Nashville, Tennessee, 1969

Moore, G.F. *Metempsychosis*, Harvard University Press, 1914

Moss, Peter, and Keeton, Joe. *Encounters with the Past*, Sidgwick & Jackson, London, 1979

M'Taggart, John. *Human Immortality and Pre-Existence*, Edward Arnold, London, 1916

Murray, Oswald. *The Spiritual Universe*, Duckworth, London, 1924

Myers, F.W.H. *Human Personality and Its Survival of Bodily Death*, Longmans, London, 1903; University Books, New York, 1961

Nayak, G.C. *Evil, Karma and Reincarnation*, Visva-Bharati University, Santiniketan, 1973

Nethercot, A.N. *The Last Four Lives of Annie Besant*, Rupert Hart-Davis, London, 1963

Nickelsburg, George W.E. *Resurrection, Immortality and Eternal Life in Intertestamental Judaism*, Harvard University Press, 1972
Nikhilananda, Swami. *Man in Search of Immortality*, Allen & Unwin, London, 1968
Nyanatiloka, Mahathera. *Karma and Rebirth*, Buddhist Publication Society, Kandy, 1959
Oesterley, W.O.E. *Immortality and the Unseen World*, SPCK, London; Macmillan, New York, 1921
Oesterreich, T.K. *Possession, Demoniacal and Other*, Kegan Paul, Trench, Trubner, London, 1930
Osborn, A.W. *The Superphysical*, Ivor Nicholson & Watson, London, 1937
Osis, Karlis. *Deathbed Observations by Doctors and Nurses*, Parapsychology Foundation, New York, 1961
Ostrander, Sheila, and Schroeder, Lynn. *PSI, Psychic Discoveries Behind the Iron Curtain*, Prentice-Hall, Englewood Cliffs, New Jersey, 1970; Sphere Books, London, 1973
Osty, E. *Supernormal Faculties in Man*, Methuen, London, 1923
Ouspensky, P.D. *The Fourth Way*, Routledge & Kegan Paul, London, 1967
Pache, René. *The Future Life*, Moody, Chicago; Marshall, Morgan & Scott, London, 1972
Parrinder, Geoffrey. *The Indestructible Soul*, Allen & Unwin, London; Barnes & Noble, New York, 1973
Pascal, Theophile. *Reincarnation: A Study of Human Evolution*, Theosophical Publishing House, London, 1965
Pear, T.H. *Remembering and Forgetting*, Methuen, London, 1949
Penelhum, Terence. *Survival and Disembodied Existence*, Routledge & Kegan Paul, London; Humanities Press, New York, 1970
Phillips, D.Z. *Death and Immortality*, Macmillan, London; St Martin's Press, New York, 1970
Phillips, Phil, and Sybil. *Is Death the End?* Corgi, London, 1972
Pieper, Josef. *Death and Immortality*, Burns & Oates, London; Herder, New York, 1968
Pike, James A. *The Other Side*, W.H. Allen, London, 1969
Podmore, Frank. *Telepathic Hallucinations*, Milner, London, 1909
Pole, W.T. *The Silent Road*, Spearman, London, 1960
Prince, Walter Franklin. *The Case of Patience Worth*, Society for Psychical Research, Boston, 1929
Pringle-Pattison, A.S. *The Idea of Immortality*, Clarendon Press, Oxford, 1922; Kraus Reprint, New York, 1971

Radhakrishnan, S. (trans. and ed.) *The Bhagavadgita*, Allen & Unwin, London, 1949; Harper & Row, New York, 1969

Rahner, Karl. *On the Theology of Death*, Burns & Oates, London, 1961; Herder, New York, 1965

Raudive, Constantin. *Breakthrough: An Amazing Experiment in Electronic Communication with the Dead*, Colin Smythe, London, 1971

Ringgren, H. (ed.). *Fatalistic Beliefs in Religion, Folklore, and Literature*, Oliver & Boyd, London, 1967

Robbins, Ann Manning. *Both Sides of the Veil*, Unwin, London, 1910

Rochas, Eugène Albert de. *Les vies successives*, Charcornac, Paris, 1924

Rouse, W.H.D. (ed.). *The Jatakas, or Stories of the Buddha's Former Births*, Oxford University Press, 1910

Royce, Josiah. *The Conception of Immortality*, Houghton Mifflin, Boston, 1900

Runciman, Steven. *The Medieval Manichee. A Study of the Christian Dualist Heresy*, Cambridge University Press, 1947

Rutter, O. *The Scales of Karma*, Rider, London, 1938

Ryall, Edward W. *Second Time Round*, with an Introduction and Appendix by Ian Stevenson, Spearman, London, 1974

Ryle, Gilbert. *The Concept of Mind*; Hutchinson, London, 1949

Sahay, K.K.N. *Reincarnation: Verified Cases of Rebirth After Death*, Sahay, Bareilly, 1927

Salter, W.H. *Zoar, or The Evidence of Psychical Research Concerning Survival*, Sidgwick & Jackson, London, 1961

Schwarz, B.E. *Parent-Child Telepathy*, Garrett, New York, 1971

Sewall, May Wright. *Neither Dead Nor Sleeping*, Watkins, London, 1921

Shepherd, A.P. *A Scientist of the Invisible*, Hodder & Stoughton, London, 1954

Sherwood, Jane. *The Country Beyond*, Rider, London, 1945

Shirley, Ralph. *The Problem of Rebirth*, Rider, London, 1940

Simon, Ulrich. *Heaven in the Christian Tradition*, Rockliff, London; Harper, New York, 1958

Singer, June. *Boundaries of the Soul*, Gollancz, London, 1973

Sinnett, A.P. *Karma and Union*, Theosophical Publishing House, London, 1900

Siwek, Paul. *The Enigma of the Hereafter*, Philosophical Library, New York, 1952

Smith, Alson J. *Immortality: The Scientific Evidence*, Signet Books, New York, 1954

Smith, W. Whately, *A Theory of the Mechanisms of Survival*, Kegan Paul, Trench, Trubner, London, 1920

Smyth, Frank (ed.). *Frontiers of Belief*, BPC Publishing Ltd., London, 1970-72

Somerlott, Robert. *Modern Occultism*, Robert Hale, London, 1972

Stearn, Jess. *Edgar Cayce. The Sleeping Prophet*, Doubleday, New York, 1967

Stearn, Jess. *The Second Life of Susan Ganier*, Frewin, London, 1968

Steiner, Rudolf. *The Manifestations of Karma*, Rudolf Steiner Press, London, 1947

Steiner, Rudolf. *Between Death and Rebirth*, 2nd ed., Rudolf Steiner Press, London, 1975

Stendahl, Krister (ed.). *Immortality and Resurrection*, Macmillan, New York, 1965

Stevenson, Ian. *The Evidence for Survival from Claimed Memories of Former Incarnations*, M.C. Peto, Tadworth, 1961

Stevenson, Ian. *Xenoglossy: A Review and Report of a Case*, Virginia University Press, Charlottesville; John Wright, Bristol, 1973

Stevenson, Ian. *Twenty Cases Suggestive of Reincarnation*, 2nd rev. ed., Virginia University Press, Charlottesville, 1974

Stewart, Ada J. *Falcon: The Autobiography of His Grace James the 4, King of Scots*, Peter Davis, London, 1970

Stone, W.C., and Browning, N.L. *The Other Side of the Mind*, Prentice-Hall, Englewood Cliffs, 1964

Story, Francis. *The Case for Rebirth*, Buddhist Publication Society, Kandy, 1935

Strawson, William. *Jesus and the Future Life*, 2nd ed., Epworth Press, London, 1970

Streeter, B.H. *Immortality*, Macmillan, London and New York, 1917

Sugrue, Thomas. *There is a River*, Henry Holt, New York, 1942

Swedenborg, Emanuel. *Heaven and Hell*, ed. by J.W. Hancock, Swedenborg Society, London, 1850

Swedenborg, Emanuel. *Heaven and Its Wonders, and Hell*, Swedenborg Foundation, New York and London, 1958

Temkin, O. *The Falling Sickness*, 2nd rev. ed., Johns Hopkins Press, Baltimore and London, 1971

Thomas, C. Drayton. *The Life Beyond Death, With Evidence*, Collins, London, 1928

Thurston, Herbert. *The Physical Phenomena of Mysticism* Burns Oates, London, 1952

Toynbee, Arnold, *et al. Man's Concern With Death*, Hodder & Stoughton, London, 1968

Tyrrell, G.N.M. *The Personality of Man*, Penguin, Harmondsworth, 1946

Underwood, Peter. *Dictionary of the Occult and Supernatural*, Fontana, Collins, London, 1979

Underwood, Peter, and Wilder, Leonard. *Lives to Remember: A Case Book on Reincarnation*, Robert Hale, London, 1975

Vasiliev, Leonid L. *Mysterious Phenomena of the Human Psyche*, University Books, New York, 1965

Veith, Ilza. *Hysteria: The History of a Disease*, Chicago University Press, 1965

Wachsmuth, Guenther. *Reincarnation*, Rudolph Steiner Press, London, 1952

Walker, Benjamin. *Beyond the Body*, Routledge & Kegan Paul, London and Boston, 1974

Walker, Benjamin. *Encyclopedia of Esoteric Man*, Routledge & Kegan Paul, London; Stein & Day, New York, 1977

Walker, D.P. *The Decline of Hell*, Routledge & Kegan Paul, London; University of Chicago Press, 1964

Walker, E.D. (ed.). *Reincarnation: A Study of Forgotten Truth*, Ward Lock, London, 1888; 2nd ed., Macoy Publication Co., New York, 1926

Wallace, Mary Bruce. *The Thinning of the Veil*, Watkins, London, 1919

Wambach, Helen. *Reliving Past Lives: The Evidence Under Hypnosis*, Hutchinson, London, 1978

Wambach, Helen. *Life Before Life*, Bantam Books, New York, 1979

Weatherhead, Leslie. *The Case for Re-Incarnation*, City Temple, London, 1957

Webb, C.C.J. *God and Personality*, Allen & Unwin, London; Macmillan, New York, 1918

Welbon, G.R. *The Buddhist Nirvana and Its Western Interpreters*, Chicago University Press, 1968

Wickland, Karl. *Thirty Years Among the Dead*, Los Angeles, 1924; reprint, Spiritualist Press, London, 1968

Wilberforce, Basil. *Spiritual Consciousness*, Stock, London, 1913
Williams, Bernard. *Problems of the Self*, Cambridge University Press, 1973
Wills, Arthur J. *Life Now and Forever*, Rider, London, 1942
Wilson, Colin. *The Occult*, Mayflower Books, London, 1973
Wood, F.H. *The Egyptian Miracle*, McKay, Philadelphia, 1940; Watkins, London, 1955
Yost, Casper S. *Patience Worth: A Psychic Mystery*, Holt, Rinehart & Winston, New York, 1916

# Index